PENGUIN BUSINESS

DESIGN YOUR CAREER

Pavan Soni is an innovation evangelist by profession and a teacher by passion. He is the founder of Inflexion Point, which offers programmes on design, innovation and leadership. He has conducted over 600 workshops with 175-plus organizations in ten countries. Apart from being an adjunct faculty at the Indian School of Business, Hyderabad, and Indian Institute of Management (IIM) Bangalore, Pavan is a columnist at *Mint*, YourStory, Inc42, *Entrepreneur* and *People Matters*. His monthly newsletter, Inflexion Point, reaches over 20,000 enthusiasts across the world. Pavan was the only Indian to be shortlisted for the prestigious 'FT & McKinsey Bracken Bower Award for the Best Business Book of the Year 2016'. He has been invited five times to speak at the TEDx, and is featured as one of the '100 Digital Influencers of 2020' by YourStory. Pavan is a gold medallist from MBM Engineering College, Jodhpur, and did his postgraduate diploma in international education from IIM Mumbai. He finished his doctoral studies from IIM Bangalore in the domain of innovation management. He is passionate about fitness, spirituality, music, chess, reading and writing. For more career advice, please visit www.pavansoni.com.

ALSO BY THE SAME AUTHOR

Design Your Thinking

DESIGN YOUR CAREER

LEAD SELF,
LEAD OTHERS,
LEAD CHANGE

PAVAN SONI

PENGUIN
BUSINESS

An imprint of Penguin Random House

PENGUIN BUSINESS

Penguin Business is an imprint of the Penguin Random House group of
companies whose addresses can be found at global.penguinrandomhouse.com

Published by Penguin Random House India Pvt. Ltd
4th Floor, Capital Tower 1, MG Road,
Gurugram 122 002, Haryana, India

First published in Penguin Business by Penguin Random House India 2024

10 9 8 7 6 5 4 3 2 1

ISBN 9780143464938

Typeset in Adobe Garamond Pro by MAP Systems, Bengaluru, India
Printed at Thomson Press India Ltd, New Delhi

www.penguin.co.in

Dedicated to my wife, Nimisha, for being my Earth,
and my daughter, Avnira, for being my Sky

Contents

Introduction

You may die accidentally, but you can't afford to *live* accidentally. You must try to live with an intent, and a design to achieve that intent. Research suggests that if you live till the age of seventy-five, you will spend at least twenty-five years sleeping. Working and preparing to work will come a close second. Increasingly though, both eight hours of sleep and eight hours of work are becoming a rarity. What you may not be realizing is that life is long, and you must learn to pace it well. There is no point in hurrying through the journey, feeling exhausted early in the game and then wondering what just happened. You need to design your life and careers consciously.

Why a book on career? Today, you are confronted with a lot of compelling career options, but with little guidance. A generation ago, retiring from your very first job was perfectly legitimate. Today, it is an exception. And in a generation from now, the very notion of jobs will undergo a drastic change. New-age engagement models—work-from-home, freelancing, gig-workforce, moonlighting, co-working spaces, solopreneur and entrepreneur-in-residence—have ushered a significant flux in both formal and informal work settings. There are opportunities galore, and the democratization of technology has only exacerbated your quest for the most suitable career. It begets that the external search must follow a deep internal search. That's what this book offers: a guide to searching within.

The book stems from self-realization and is directed at helping others in that cause. Over the past twenty years, I have been lucky enough to engage with thousands of working professionals across levels and industries. The distillation of my 550 workshops at over 175 organizations across five countries is this: human talent is grossly underutilized. There is nothing worse than a wasted talent. Organizational politics, a culture of mistrust, an urge to please superiors, a constant struggle to be relevant, a sense of self-doubt and frequent organizational restructuring result in cardinal waste of talent. The least that can be done is to offer some hope and clarity to individuals who feel helpless amid all the chaos, and to give them the appropriate tools and frameworks to guide their careers towards fulfilment. This book is a humble attempt in that direction.

Who is this book for? A better question still will be: Who is this book not for? It is not for somebody uninterested in leading a gratifying career. A student, an entrepreneur, a working executive, a teacher, a freelancer, a business leader, a homemaker and even a politician will be keen on well-designed utilization of time and talent, in the pursuit of a worthwhile goal. Essentially, a career is a means of marshalling your precious time and talent towards a meaningful outcome—meaningful not just to self, but also to the larger milieu. And this invokes the difficult task of thinking through. Alas, we don't pay much attention to thinking, for it's assumed that we get better at thinking with more of it. But certainly, akin to any other skill, thinking can also be honed with effort. This book helps you think better to make more conscious choices in life and in your career.

This book is not about your workplace or those around you. Rather, it is about you. If you read this book from a narrow aperture of what to apply on a Monday morning, you will be sorely disappointed. But if your intent is to absorb this discourse from a holistic perspective, you will not only be a better thinker but also a highly valuable asset, wherever you are. This book coaches you on how to discover your interests, systematically analyse your options, take tough decisions, navigate uncertainties, course correct and inspire others to follow their passions, meaningfully. One note on passion, though: passion is blind. More on this later.

The book has six chapters, each offering a specific insight on how to shape your thinking and harness it to build a rewarding career—as an individual contributor, as a manager and as a leader. Each chapter has sub-sections detailing key concepts, with associated models and relevant examples.

The first chapter—**Life Is Long, Pace It Well**—sets the tone of this book. Popular media has hurried us into thinking that if we don't arrive in life by the age of forty and retire thereafter, we are no good. But I haven't come across anybody who's retired happily at forty! Have you? Most people continue to work for a meaningful career. The chapter offers insights on how to know your prime movers in life, to slow down, focus on the vital few and the major things and shrink your zone of concern to elevate your impact on things that count. It will help you realize that while a year may pass by, a lot can be achieved in a decade, provided you keep walking.

The second chapter—**Deserve before Your Desire**—pushes you into thinking about the future and whether you have the competence and attitude to remain relevant over the long haul. Of greatest importance is the preservation of your attention. How do you pay attention to your attention? This chapter elucidates the significance of compassion and empathy, while building a case of bounded empathy. The future belongs to those who can create and not just manage; this calls for sharpening curiosity, fluid identity and being disciplined. There's a section on the importance of hobbies and how you must protect those from your profession, lest you become a bot. You need to have a rich life outside of your working hours which can offer you meaning, emotional stability, social relevance, personal vitality and a knack of connecting the dots in different dimensions.

The third chapter—**Own Your Career, or Somebody Else Will**—nudges you into taking care of your body and mind and treating them as an asset to be nurtured instead of a resource to be exploited. What's the fun of dragging an ailing body through a long life? This chapter is a call for identifying your passion, creating a portfolio of enterprise, working hard but tinkering along the way, the pursuit of financial freedom and how to hone an enterprising attitude. Of special importance is the choice of when and how to pursue your entrepreneurial dreams with courage. In a career spanning over forty years, you can't leave much to chance. And while things may not always go as per plan, you can't afford not to plan. Because plans can fail, but planning doesn't.

The fourth chapter—**Focus on High Leverage Activities**—brings you to the heart of personal and professional excellence. A high leverage activity is one which, if done today, will offer you exponential returns in the future. By relooking at the time-tested Urgency-Importance Matrix, you will understand how to steal time from busy matters to create enduring assets, whereby reclaiming your time. You will learn that knowledge is not power and that time is not money. That technology is a great slave but an awful master. And if you know how to tame technology to your strategy, then only you can create a significantly superior future. You learn how to delegate effectively, solve complex problems well and narrate stories to move minds and hearts.

The fifth chapter—**Think Strategically, Act Decisively**—reminds you that the quality of your life is defined by the quality of your thinking. There are people who get confused about the smallest of matters, and then there are those who make life-defining moves without a second thought. The latter have trained their heuristics through the rigour of thinking slow and deep. This chapter presents research-backed and practically grounded insights on how to think the big picture, and to take a future-back, outside-in approach to decision-making; the importance of mental models and ways to create one for yourself; the means of making trade-offs, being politically savvy and maintaining a knowledge differential. You need to avoid complicating your thinking. This chapter is an antidote to that phenomenon.

The last chapter—**Leadership Is a Choice Not Everyone Can Make**—raises the discussion from leading self to leading others and establishments. Just because you got promoted in your career doesn't mean that your thinking got promoted, too. You may still be thinking very much from where you started. Leaders have a soul in the game and not just their skin. They offer their teams air cover while they experiment vigorously. They focus on honing a climate of innovation by designing asymmetric incentives and yet are vulnerable by choice. These and many more practices on how to lead high talent density teams, whether as entrepreneurs or corporate leaders. Leadership is not a title, it's a way of life.

The book gleans insights from the realms of history, psychology, sociology, medicine, politics, sports, military, business, economics, arts, music, entertainment and spirituality to offer you a nudge on how to think better, live better and make an impact on people around you. We wrap up the book with an **Appendix** presenting some quotable quotes that can possibly move you and others.

Here's one for starters.

Imagine you are a woodcutter. And you have a target of how many logs of wood are to be chopped in a given day. As you are busy chopping wood, you discover that your axe has got blunt and that you must increasingly put in more effort to meet your target. You know that you must sharpen the axe but you won't, for the fear of falling behind on numbers. If only you stop chopping the wood can you afford to sharpen your axe and possibly increase your productivity and effectiveness. This book is about sharpening your axe. Please don't chop any more wood before you finish reading this one.

1

Life Is Long, Pace It Well

'Nothing ever happened in the past that can prevent you from being present now.'

—Eckhart Tolle[1]

Michelangelo di Lodovico Buonarroti Simoni, the Italian sculptor, painter, architect and poet of the Renaissance period, lived till the ripe age of eighty-eight. Leonardo da Vinci, sixty-seven. Isaac Newton, eighty-four. Charles Darwin, seventy-three. Thomas Edison, eighty-four. Rabindranath Tagore, eighty. Albert Einstein, seventy-six. Pablo Picasso, ninety-one. Stephen Hawking, seventy-six. Confucius is said to have lived till the age of seventy-two, Socrates touched seventy-one, and Siddhartha Gautama was going strong into his 1980s. These were some of the most influential figures in the realms of spirituality, science, art, literature and technology. They not only created history but also recreated themselves along the way. They paced their lives well enough that they left an indelible impression on generations to come.

I may sound biased, of presenting you with a selective view. Let's look at another list. Alexander the Great, thirty-two. Wolfgang Amadeus Mozart, thirty-five. Vincent van Gogh, thirty-seven. Bruce Lee, thirty-two. Paul Kalanithi, thirty-seven (check him out). Swami Vivekananda, thirty-nine. And, of course, Heath Ledger, the quintessential Joker of *Dark Knight,* twenty-eight. As for the *Dark Knight*, the genius Christopher Nolan shipped it all by his thirty-seventh birthday. Not to forget the 27 Club, comprising musical legends like Kurt Cobain, Brian Jones, Jim Morrison, Amy Winehouse, Robert Johnson, Janis Joplin, Jimi Hendrix and others who died at age twenty-seven. The good news is that I and, perhaps, you have outlived all these people, but the bad news is that it hasn't amounted to much.

What I am hinting at is that life need not be long, but if it is, then you must be sure that you are not rushing through it. Common across the two lists is the clarity of purpose and the reinvention of the methods. Some get it early and sign off, and yet others make it count by leading a life of relevance and reverence, being busy chipping at their calling late into the evening. For them, life be a lamp that glows well into the dark of the night rather than a spark that burns quickly and bright.

Between 1950 and 2020, the life expectancy of Indians has grown from thirty-seven years to above seventy years.[2] The question is: *What are we doing with these extra years?* Many of the aforementioned people lived at a time when plagues and diseases were quite common, some of the most rudimentary medical aids were still decades away, and yet they managed to offer profound insights and world-changing creations. In contrast, are we putting our excess to good use? We are living a lot longer, but are we living it well? Are we living by design, or by chance?

You must have heard people saying, 'I want to retire by the age of forty, and then travel the world.' Yet others justify their hectic pace claiming that they are busy saving the world. But how many people have you come across who have bid adieu to their work by their forties? I have not. In fact, I have read about those who suffered a massive cardiac arrest in their early forties. Even the ace sportspeople, who always knew how short their career was, had plans on how to keep going well into the twilight. It's not easy to let go. Then why not pace it well?

As Phil Knight, the creator of Nike and a passionate runner, reflects, 'There is a primal urge to compare everything—life, business, adventures of all sorts—to a race. But the metaphor is often inadequate. It can take you only so far.'[3] And yet, 'Just Do It' seems to be the rally cry. College students want to make it big before their final year, corporate executives often double up as part-time entrepreneurs, talented homemakers don't get tired tracking likes and shares on their latest Insta posts, and so goes the nervous energy chasing the next. You don't realize that if you have another fifty years, what's the point in getting tired so fast and then dragging yourself the rest of the way.

Let me throw up some surprises.

You may assume that the most successful entrepreneurs are school or college dropouts and that they max out in their early twenties. On the contrary, research suggests that the prime age for successful founders is forty-five and not twenty-five. Based on a study of 2.7 million people who founded businesses between 2007–14, researchers at MIT discovered that the average age of founders for high-tech employment, VC-backed firms and patenting firms is forty-three, forty-two and forty-five, respectively. Interestingly, Steve Jobs and Bill Gates started Apple and Microsoft, respectively, in their early twenties, but their stocks peaked when both were in their forties.[4] It seems that the mad rush out of college and into the office of investors among the twenty-somethings is suicidal, for you would rather have a proper education that puts you in good stead for a longish career.

Let's look at science. At what age do you think scientists perform their Nobel Prize-winning work: twenties, thirties or forties? Rasmus Bjørk, a researcher at the Technical University of Denmark, analysed every awarded Nobel Prize since 1995 for Physics and Economics, since 2000 for Chemistry and since 2006 for Physiology or Medicine. The prize-winning work for scientists peaked at age 44.1±9.7 years. Those in Physics bloomed earlier than those in Chemistry or Biology.[5] Once again, we hit the mid-forties.

So, if you haven't yet 'arrived' in life as you are reading this book, you are in rather large and good company. What matters is that you are not burning yourself chasing a moving target, measured on externally dictated yardsticks. Slow down, my friend. Slow down, for Khalil Gibran says, 'You work that you keep pace with the earth and the soul of the earth.'[6] Instead, look at what the rapidity of pace has done to our lives and Mother Nature. We owe it to our grandchildren to slow down.

For the uninitiated, this is what slowing down looks like. Reflected Bruce Lee:[7]

Live content with small means; seek elegance rather than luxury, and refinement rather than fashion. Be worthy, not respectable, wealthy, not rich; study hard, think quietly, talk gently, act frankly; bear all cheerfully, do all bravely, await occasions, hurry never.

Hurry never. Here's how.

Know your prime mover

To understand yourself is the beginning of wisdom, said Jiddu Krishnamurti.[8] And yet, understanding oneself is a life-consuming exercise. As per Bruce Lee, one of Krishnamurti's disciples, 'All knowledge is self-knowledge.'[9] So, let's start with understanding ourselves.

What is a prime mover? Physically speaking, a prime mover is an initial source of motivation. It could be a windmill, waterwheel, turbine or an internal combustion engine. In the context of human beings, there could practically be four prime movers: Fear, Greed, Duty and Love.

Fear: I do it, or else . . .
Greed: I do it, so that . . .
Duty: I must do it.
Love: I just do it.

Fear is the most primitive driver. It manifests in our fight or flight instinct, which hasn't left us through the eons of evolution. It is palpable even in unruly traffic and office meetings. Fear is a great motivator, for we can achieve the unthinkable, often out of sheer self-preservation. The fear of becoming irrelevant pushes several celebrities to hit the treadmill, take up painful surgeries, survive on experimental diets and keep a cheerful demeanour. But the ugly reality is that fear is exhausting; it is tiring, and one can't have that as one's perpetual drive. It burns us up.

Next comes greed. That quick and often unconscious graduation from needs to wants to desires. We want water, for we are thirsty and as soon as we are satiated, we want juice or some exotic food, and then it doesn't take much before we see ourselves desiring indefinitely—a new car . . . the list goes on. Most of the corporate progress, pan-hierarchy, is largely attributed to greed. Greed is an abyss, always leaving one thirsty.

A sense of duty is still noble. It keeps us going. We may have that self-righteousness or concern for our employer, team, employees, nation or even humanity. It's a bargain where we are willing to endure, as long as we can seek something valuable coming our way. Several parents take care of their children predominantly from an 'I must' standpoint, and that kind of parenting is often lauded. Entrepreneurs work hard to keep their 'baby' afloat, soldiers don't dodge a bullet for their responsibility, and so does the surgeon who stands for over eight hours for a treacherous operation. But then, there is a reciprocity which must be honoured.

But how about doing something out of sheer love? While fear may burn us up, greed may turn us on and duty may seem banal after a time, it's love that will keep us going, as one will do it for the very act and not really the consequence. Though that may seem idealistic, we have examples of artists, scientists and others who have transcended the boundaries of pain and glory to leave something behind, of parents who just love waiting for their children right outside the school, or a street artist oblivious to the humdrum around her. That's pious and without any expiry date. Love liberates. Love inspires. Love is enduring and vastly meaningful.

Don't be mistaken that every time we must have love driving us around. It doesn't have to, for it's better that way. If I look at working on this book, I have all four drivers at play. I fear 'What if the book doesn't do well, or I am unable to meet my publisher's deadline?' I have a greed of becoming a bestselling author. Working with the editorial team and going through the motions of publishing the book is a duty that I must perform. But writing the book, researching for it, revising it, sorting my thoughts—all that I love. And because I love the core process to the very core, everything else can be managed. Nothing hurts. The day I cease to love reading, writing and teaching, the rest will loom large and inundate me. The task is to seek love as a driver amid our fears, longings and responsibilities, whether it's work or life.

Even when Nobel laureates have no financial or legal obligations to teach, they still do—for the love of it. Contrasting to the other great theoretical physicists of the time ruminating at the prestigious Institute for Advanced Study at Princeton, Richard Feynman chose to stay back at Caltech. 'In any thinking process there are moments when everything is going good and you've got wonderful ideas,' concedes Feynman. 'Teaching is an interruption, and so it's the greatest pain in the neck in the world. And then there are the *longer* periods of time when not much is coming to you. You're not getting any ideas, and if you're doing nothing at all, it drives you nuts! You can't even say "I'm teaching my class" . . . So I find that teaching and the students keep life going, and I would *never* accept any position in which somebody has invented a happy situation for me where I don't have to teach. Never.'[10] He loved teaching, and the rest happened.

If we do something out of love, we can overcome hardships, and we don't seek external validation. An instructive episode comes from the life of Bruce Lee. When he was confined to bed rest for six months owing to a back injury, Lee utilized the opportunity to compile his training methods and philosophical thoughts into several volumes of text. The more famous ones being *Striking Thoughts*, *Bruce Lee—Artist of Life*, and *Jeet Kune Do—Bruce Lee's Commentaries on the Martial Way*. Such motivations can't emerge from fear, greed or even duty. There must be love, lest we get frustrated.

The pandemic was the first time when scores of professionals were pushed into investigating within. When millions of office-goers, college-goers and generally out-goers were pushed to stay at home, they went crazy. Suddenly, we were forced to confront ourselves. Several resorted to media and social media, yet others risked law and order to step out, and a few stepped within. They, for the first time, perhaps, listened to their inner calling, their love, away from the fear, greed and duties that occupied the conscious thus far. It helped many to identify and acknowledge their passion in life and offered an excuse to follow it.

When in 1665 the bubonic plague broke out in England, twenty-two-year-old Isaac Newton, then studying at Cambridge University, left for his farm home at Woolsthorpe, some sixty miles north of the university. Over the next two years, in total solitude, Newton would formulate the principles of universal gravitation, invent a new field in Mathematics—Calculus—further Geometry, and discover the composition of light, among other scientific achievements.[11] His prime years of scientific productivity were almost jeopardized by the plague, but the arduous Newton didn't let that happen. He turned an adversity into an opportunity, for he was ready and self-aware. By the time he was twenty-five, he had already established himself as one of the most important scientific figures in the whole of history, and then he indulged in Alchemy and Theology, his new-found loves.

His love of poetry, literature, teaching and experimenting supported A.P.J. Kalam well into his twilight years. As if Padma Bhushan, Padma Vibhushan and Bharat Ratna were not enough, Kalam authored twelve books, while teaching and leading on the sidelines. And how did he die? On 27 July 2015, while delivering a lecture at IIM Shillong, he collapsed on stage due to a cardiac arrest. He lived doing what he loved, and he died the same way. (I wish I get that kind of a death). Kalam lived till the ripe age of eighty-three, gave us satellites, missiles and nuclear tests, became India's People's President, and ignited young minds, never in any hurry.

Slowing down, thinking deeply and picking wisely on what drives us is the key to effective living. It turns out that we often discover our prime movers when nothing else seems to be going well in our lives—when we are by ourselves. Nehru, Gandhi, Mandela and Frankl, all did their best writing while in prisons. We certainly don't need to wait for such exigencies. Rather, keep investigating about what drives us and then move towards it slowly.

Where are 'you' in the whole scheme of things?

6 July 2008, the Centre Court, All England Club, London: That's the Men's Final of the Wimbledon, the most

prestigious tennis tournament in the world. At the centre we have the five-time Wimbledon champion, Roger Federer, facing the world number two, Rafael Nadal. While Federer plays for history, Nadal aims at redemption, after having lost the last two finals to the master at the very same venue. Touted as the most famous and longest match in the game's history, the 2008 final lasted for four hours and forty-eight minutes, with neither of the champions willing to give away anything. Interrupted by rain and well beyond 9 p.m., the match defined both Federer and Nadal. More importantly, it gave birth to Nadal, the champion—the man who stared at retirement from tennis at nineteen, owing to a grave foot injury.

This is a story about isolating yourself from the world, to be able to be at peak performance, enduring physical pain, external noise and living entirely in the moment. As Nadal admits, 'Because what I battle hardest to do in a tennis match is to quiet the voices in my head, to shut everything out of my mind but the contest itself and concentrate every atom of my being on the point I am playing.' The Spaniard maintains, 'It is the player . . . who manages to isolate himself best from his fears and from the ups and downs in morale a match inevitably brings, who ends up being world number one.'[12]

To get to grips with it, let's have a look at how the day panned out for Nadal.

All through the Wimbledon, Rafael stays with his family and friends at a rented house right across the All England Club. This lets him concentrate and cut down on any distraction, including travel. He cooks his own food and prefers a simple pasta and fish. A night before, Nadal plays darts with his coach and friends, and watches a few movies before managing a short nap. At breakfast, he has cereal, orange juice and a milk chocolate drink (never coffee), and some home-made bread sprinkled with salt and olive oil. It is followed by massages and warming up before the match. Then come the layers of bandages and shots of injections to his troubling left foot to numb it down for him to endure the match. And then the most important of them all: a cold shower. 'I do this before every match,' writes Nadal in his memoir, *Rafa*. 'Under the cold shower I enter a new space in which I feel my power and resilience grow. I'm a different man when I emerge. I'm activated. I'm in "the flow".'[13]

If you wish to pace your life, you must learn to isolate yourself from the vagaries of the world. Peak performance comes from clear priorities, and at the centre it is—you. Then comes the rest. The very Nadal who ferociously guards his personal space declares, 'I build a wall around myself when I play, but my family is the cement that holds the wall together.'[14] To the outside world, he is inscrutable, and most achievers prefer it that way.

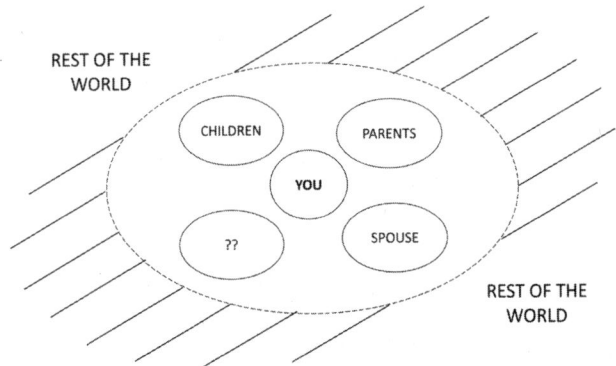

Figure 1: Knowing your place and others in your world.

Figure 1 attempts to offer clarity on priorities in life. It must start with You. Don't think you owe it to anybody. Your life is your struggle, face it, own it, fully. Not even your parents, children, spouse, friends, or anybody else can take that place. You bear the consequences of your choices. The sooner you realize it, the better it's for you. Most parents work all their lives for their children, or so they say, and in the process their health suffers, they let go of things they wanted to pursue, and in the end when their children make it, the same parents are often filled with bitterness. They feel let down, short-changed, for they 'sacrificed' themselves to offer a better life to their offspring, and the progeny doesn't seem to care.

Whose fault? Parents'. Nobody asked them, least of all their children, to sacrifice themselves. More importantly, what lesson are you offering to your children? You do the same as you grow up, and ad infinitum. Instead, if you took care of your health, your ambitions, your personality, your gifts and grit, you send a strong message to your children Have a life of your own! I took this extreme example to drive home the point that nobody, absolutely nobody, deserves to take that central position. If you allow that displacement, you are preparing yourself for disappointment and others for abuse.

Next comes the second orbit that comprises your parents, spouse, children, and '??'. Your parents give life, the spouse shapes your life and the children sustain that life. You can fill this fourth spot with any of your siblings, friends, teachers, colleagues, co-founders, students or anybody who's truly at the same level as the preceding three entities—parents, spouse and children. But be very selective, for *every tie costs*.

Here's what Indra Nooyi, the first and only female CEO of PepsiCo, wrote in her farewell letter: 'Finally, think hard about time. We have so little of it on this earth. Make the most of your days and make the space for the loved ones who matter most. Take it from me. I've been blessed with an amazing career, but if I'm being honest, there have been moments I wish I'd spent more time with my children and family. So, I encourage you: be mindful of your choices on the road ahead.'[15]

How did the mother of two, Indra Nooyi, shape PepsiCo as its head? Soon after Indra was appointed as the CEO, in 2006, she brought her full self to bearing. One of her concerns as a mother was the sugar, fat and salt content in sodas and chips, the staples of PepsiCo. Further, growing up in Chennai, she had experienced acute water shortage and was fully aware that right from washing of bottles to filling them with carbonated drinks, PepsiCo was consuming huge amounts of fresh water, not to mention the plastic waste generated by its fast-moving products. As a mother and one from a developing country, she had a choice to make: Should she choose short-term returns over long-term gains, or initiate a large-scale transformation at the company, which was going pretty well by most standards? She chose the latter.

Under the *Performance with Purpose* (PwP) initiative, Indra identified three product categories at PepsiCo: *Fun for You*, *Better for You* and *Good for You*. The *Fun for You* category comprised the colas and chips, the *Better for You* had baked products and low calorie beverages, whereas the *Good for You* had oats, juices, water and other healthy options. She hired Mehmood Khan from Takeda Pharmaceuticals to lead corporate R&D and Mauro Porcini from 3M to head design. And together, they worked on new products, new formats and new customer experiences. Apart from topping various charts on environment and sustainability, by 2017, almost 50 per cent of the company's portfolio was *Better for You* and *Good for You*. That's real transformation. And it's all because Indra chose to listen to herself, and care for her inner orbit.

What happens when you make time for yourself? You get to contemplate and create. As is evident from the reflections of the great inventor, Nikola Tesla.

'From my childhood I was compelled to concentrate attention upon myself,' reflets Tesla. 'This caused me much suffering, but to my present view, it was a blessing in disguise for it taught me to appreciate the inestimable value of introspection in the preservation of life, as well as means of achievement.'[16] Tesla was not known as a great collaborator, but like most geniuses before him, he liked being lost in his thoughts. When Thomas Edison hired Tesla to improve his DC generation plants, Tesla poured himself into the task. Working daily from 10.30 a.m. till 5 a.m., Tesla almost single-handedly brought about remarkable improvements on the generation system, before going on to invent the AC motor and developing the AC generation and transmission technology.

From age five, Elon Musk, the modern-day Edison, would be focused on a single task for long durations of time and be able to visualize what's stated in words. It was almost like an engineering drawing being formed in his mind. 'It seems as though the part of the brain that's usually reserved for visual processing—the part that is used to process images coming in from my eyes—gets taken over by internal thought processes,' explains Musk. 'For images and numbers, I can process their inter-relationships and algorithmic relationships. Acceleration, momentum, kinetic energy—how those sorts of things will be affected by objects comes through very vividly.'[17] There is little doubt how he could help build rockets at SpaceX by merely reading books.

It is only when you choose to slow down that you go inside and then explore your uniqueness and your unique calling. And yet you mostly want to *be* somebody else. At birth, you were unlike any other—including the ones born before or after you, from the same womb. And what followed thereafter was an effort to institutionalize you. First, with the 'tips of effective parenting', then the assembly lines at schools and colleges, and eventually the societal and economic forces. All your idiosyncrasies are blunted till you become predictable and 'harmless'. Only those who persevere against such forces move the world. It takes a certain attitude to identify one's uniqueness and fortitude to exploit it. And we do have a few role models here.

You are not so much unique outside-in, as much as inside-out. Your brain is unlike mine, by design. That's a fact corroborated by one of the foremost neurosurgeons in the world, George Ojemann. In the late 1980s, Ojemann combined the brain maps of 117 patients that he had operated on and came up with a startling finding: no two brains had the same location for specific functions. He concluded, 'There was substantial individual variability in the exact location of language function, some of which correlated with the patient's sex and verbal intelligence. These features were present for patients as young as 4 years and as old as 80 years, and for those with lesions acquired in early life or adulthood.'[18] We are indeed different. So why not make the most of it and run a race of our liking.

Starting age twenty-six, the German composer and pianist Ludwig van Beethoven suffered hearing loss. Before he was forty-four, Beethoven was completely deaf and yet he could compose scintillating music purely out of his imagination. This eighteenth century composer would sit at the piano, put a pencil in his mouth and touch the other end of it to the soundboard of the instrument, to feel the vibrations of the notes.[19] Deafness was not to deter his ambitions or productivity. His stellar output comprised 722 works, including nine symphonies, thirty-five piano sonatas and sixteen string quartets, spanning forty-five years.[20] That's knowing yourself and shaping your life.

Sir Richard Branson acknowledged that his dyslexia helped him take inordinate risks in life and become a rule-breaking 400-company strong entrepreneur. His daredevil stunts led him to certain death some seventy-five times, and yet none of his ventures have ever gone bankrupt. As the billionaire reflects on his learning difficulties as a child, he admits, 'The fact that I was dyslexic meant that, from a very young age, I found fantastic people to surround myself with. It taught me to delegate. I think that, by and large, dyslexics are more creative and good at seeing the bigger picture. We do think slightly differently to other people.'[21]

The ability to radically cut down the chatter outside and within your head is the hallmark of disciplined living. You can *choose* to slow down only when you are in control of your life. Be selective on the dimensions that seek your attention and efforts—the first orbit, which is You. Then comes the second orbit: those extremely close to you. And for the rest, learn to ignore profusely, tolerate comfortably and confront selectively.

Ignore, tolerate, and then confront selectively

Ignorance is bliss, goes the saying. And this can't be more virtuous than in the present age when you are bombarded with so much in so little time that feeling overwhelmed is quite natural. But you can engineer ignorance into your life, or the corollary—you can choose to be very selective—by design. As Nikola Tesla suggested: The smarter you are, the more selective you become.

So, here is a recipe of becoming selective: ITC. ITC stands for Ignore, Tolerate and Confront.

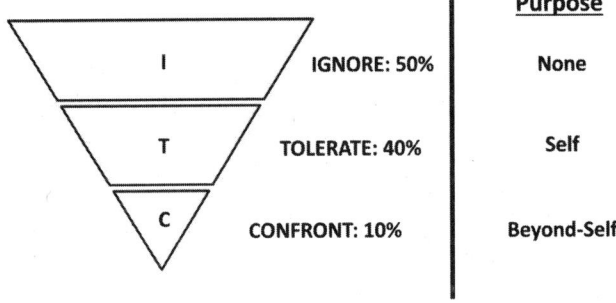

Figure 2: The ITC rule of being extremely selective.

As shown in Figure 2, it all starts with *Ignore*. There is so much happening around you—at office, at home, on twenty-four-hour news channels (they create news!) and on social media—that you can quickly get inundated. A sure recipe for feeling miserable is to watch any twenty-four-hour news channel for just an hour. The so called 'breaking news' will make you doubt your sanity. It's best to develop a healthy capacity to ignore 50 per cent of the stuff that comes along your way.

Simply ignore almost half of what you encounter on a day-to-day basis, and move on.

How about people? Should you ignore them as well? Certainly not. Appreciate that most people behave as per their current circumstances, where we often blame it on their very nature. That's what the dean of behavioural psychology, Daniel Kahneman, calls the 'fundamental attribution error'. So, when you come across someone despicable, be sure to ignore the *behaviour* and not the person. The person will turn around, soon after. Don't ignore people, just ignore their idiosyncrasies. 'Nonreaction to the ego in others is one of the most effective ways not only of going beyond ego in yourself but also of dissolving the collective human ego,' observed the spiritual guru Eckhart Tolle.[22]

Next comes *Tolerate*. If you can't ignore a situation, then you must learn to tolerate stuff which is of a higher frequency and impact. If you don't like a plot or a person and you have a choice of removing yourself from there, please do so. However, you are not always that fortunate. So, you must develop the capacity to tolerate. You must raise your threshold of engagement, and by doing so, you develop some new skills. The difference between ignoring and tolerating is *purpose*. You tolerate a certain behavior because there is something *beyond* the behavior.

Your parents or teachers pushing you towards discipline, your spouse urging you to be more sincere, your children demanding your interest in their interests—all this calls for tolerance and action. Because the stakes are high. And since you have already ignored a good 50 per cent, you can now choose to mind another sizable 40 per cent. But there is a limit to tolerating, for you don't change the world this way.

Finally, you must *Confront*. You confront selectively. You lock your horns only when you are certain that you can alter the state, or else it's better to fall back to Ignore or Tolerate. You pick your battles wisely. Answer this: How many people have you managed to change in your entire life? I guess that would be one: just you. It is only you who changes. You think you change others, but not really. It's the situation that transforms people, and the best you can do is to create the appropriate conditions or the incentives to bring about change. Hence, you should engage very selectively.

I will give Confront no more than 10 per cent. If you think you should confront more often, then you are just being too full of yourself. You are playing God. An earnest question is: Should you always ignore or tolerate before you confront? No, not always. If your boss touches you inappropriately, you don't first ignore and tolerate. You straight away confront, and confront well. But for that you must conserve your energy and emotions by ignoring a whole lot of other stuff.

When to adopt these approaches? You ignore when you can't see a purpose beyond ego satisfaction. Massaging your ego or somebody else's is a futile activity, for the returns are temporary, at best. If you see a personal purpose, of self-improvement, then tolerance is the way. Something that makes you stronger, emotionally and physically, preserves a crucial relationship or builds your character must be endured. Finally, if you have a bigger calling, of that beyond the self—much like Gandhi did when thrown out of the moving train in South Africa, or the courageous tale of Malala Yousafzai—you confront. You confront, for you are convinced that ignorance or tolerance is not a choice, and there's much more at stake than your puny ego or immediate gratification. But at any rate, keep confrontation relatively small, for it's an exhausting act.

To get a clearer perspective on this, let's take a peep into the career of Bear Grylls, of *Man vs Wild* fame. Grylls' overture in the British military as a 'blade' with the 21 SAS ended abruptly in 1996 when he was involved in a free fall parachuting accident in Kenya. He broke three vertebrae, was almost paralyzed, and was bedridden for days. At twenty-two, his career was almost finished. But he bounced back and bounced back strong. His first outing was to climb Mt Ama Dablam, which Sir Edmund Hillary described as 'unclimbable'. He made it in the very first attempt. And then the Everest. Grylls got some confidence going.

Along the way, Grylls discovered that he *loves* adventure. But he didn't know how to make money out of it. He didn't know what to call himself: a survivalist, a bushcraft guy, a climber, a skydiver. There was no script of a show on survival skills. Nothing to imitate or fall back on. Not to mention the risk of losing it all with a single accident. 'So on one hand I knew I had to keep pushing, keep risking, keep innovating, keep earning my living and building a career in this unusual way, but I was also becoming ever more aware of my own survival limitations,' admits Grylls.[23]

And in 2006, out came *Man vs Wild* and became a massive hit around the world. It ran for seven seasons over five years, and then abruptly Grylls decided to start his own venture, much to the chagrin of Discovery Channel. In 2014, Grylls had his second act, *Running Wild with Bear Grylls*, which featured celebrities ranging from superstar Rajanikanth to President Barack Obama. And this time, Grylls was the boss. In the interim, Bear Grylls ignored the naysayers, tolerated physical and emotional injuries, confronted the camera and the world, and showed us true grit.

As a side note, I would encourage you to check out these two short movie clips (a full indulgence is recommended). The first is *The Big Lebowski* (1998). There is a famous 'Bowling with the Jesus' scene, where our man, the Dude (Jeff Bridges), responds to an earful of insult nonchalantly with, 'That's just like, your opinion, man.'[24] The second is *Troy* (2004) and its famous fight scene where Achilles (Brad Pit) kills Boagrius, the hulk of an opponent, with one single, decisive blow without engaging in any fist fight, or war cry, or even a celebration.[25] That's your power of selective confrontation. You ignore it all, and then you won't.

We delve deeper into this ITC principle later when we talk about the *Zone of Concern* and the *Zone of Influence,* and the significance of the *flow channel.* For now, let's talk dermatology: the importance of thick skin.

Hone a thick skin

Success is a lousy teacher, maintains Bill Gates. Indeed, failure is instructive, but who wants to fail? How many can tolerate multiple failures and persist in the face of internal resistance and external ridicule? And yet, the ability to take on insult seems to be the key to pacing your life at your own terms.

When the world is rushing past you, your ability to remain grounded and to be selective in your response stems from three factors: a clear head, a deep heart, and a thick skin. Figure 3 depicts the three dimensions: a clear head to prioritize, a deep heart to empathize and a thick skin to materialize.

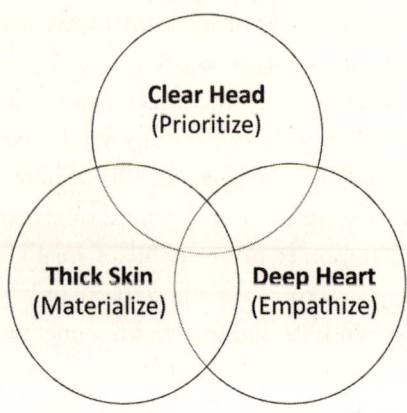

Figure 3: The triad of pacing our life well.

A *clear head* is about knowing what *not* to do. Most inventors, artists, sportspeople, scientists and celebrated entrepreneurs tend to maintain a clear head. They are very good at saying 'no'. Their threshold of engagement is high. On his return to Apple in 1997, Steve Jobs famously proclaimed, 'focusing is about saying no'.[26] Jobs cut down the product range from over two dozen to only four: one desktop and one portable device aimed at both consumers and professionals. Even today, Apple has the narrowest product range for any company of its size.

You displease a lot of people when you say 'no', but only then do you do something monumental. When Jack Welch demanded his business units be number one or two in their industry or be sold, he was demonstrating clear-headedness. He saved GE from being non-competitive in several domains and helped prepare the conglomerate for the new millennium. The 2022 split of GE into three entities, focused on aviation, healthcare and energy, is a manifestation of Welch's logic. Explains GE CEO Larry Culp, 'By creating three industry-leading, global public companies, each can benefit from greater focus, tailored capital allocation, and strategic flexibility to drive long-term growth and value.'[27] The key operative here is focus.

Being clear-headed demands thinking through the consequences, and that's where a deep heart comes into bearing. A *deep heart* is about sensitivity to the weak signals, to the unsaid, to the underdogs. It's about sifting through the chaos and clutter to pick that nugget which most others would miss out on. You need to listen well, park your judgement, have a keen sense of observation and, above all, offer people around you psychological safety. A deep heart demonstrates empathy. 'Empathy is an existential priority for a business,' opines Microsoft's turnaround CEO, Satya Nadella. In a conversation with David Rubenstein, Nadella reveals how his life taught him to become more empathetic and that's one skill which made him a better CEO.[28]

And finally, the *thick skin*. It's your ability to withstand criticism, take on blows on the way to executing an idea, the vigour with which you overcome internal doubts and external upheavals. Thick skin is what Tata Group's chairman, Natarajan Chandrasekaran (Chandra), demonstrated when he pulled the plug on the Tata Nano project. Being his pet project, Ratan Tata, the former chairman, found it extremely difficult to cut down the losses, but Chandra operated from the position of dispassion, arguing, 'I needed to stop the bleeding.'[29]

A combination of clear head, deep heart and thick skin is rare, and so is excellence. I guess the defining feature is thick skin. You must be okay with rejections. If you are risking attempting even a slight amount of creativity, be ready to be ridiculed, for a swath of people derive their self-worth from the status quo which you are attempting to alter. Criticism is the fuel of creative work. As the author Elizabeth Gilbert puts it, 'If I am allowed to speak my inner truth, then my critics are allowed to speak their inner truths, as well.'[30] Fair point.

To appreciate the interplay of deep heart, clear head and thick skin, let's revisit the history of medicine. Ever heard of Ignaz Semmelweis? Not many have, but this doctor has arguably made the most significant contribution to the science of healthcare. In 1847, Semmelweis was practicing medicine at the Vienna General Hospital. As an assistant professor, his duties included supervising difficult deliveries, teaching the students obstetrics and keeping records. The hospital had two maternity clinics—the First Clinic with a child mortality rate of about 10 per cent, mostly due to puerperal fever; and the Second Clinic averaging at 4 per cent infant mortality rate. The surprising fact was that the clinic with higher mortality rate was attended to by doctors, whereas in the other clinic, midwives assisted in deliveries. Semmelweis was puzzled why a lot more children and mothers died in the hands of trained doctors than midwives. The situation was so bad that women would prefer giving births on streets than getting admitted to the First Clinic.

After ruling out causes such as the difference in procedures or overcrowding across the two clinics, Semmelweis narrowed down the investigation to the individuals who worked there. The First Clinic served as a teaching facility for the medical students, whereas the Second Clinic was meant for instructions to midwives. By studying the routines of medical students and doctors, Semmelweis drew a hypothesis that perhaps students carried 'cadaverous particles' on their hands from the autopsy room as they later assisted deliveries. And that led to the infections and puerperal fever. But what evidence did he have? The germ theory was still years away and doctors weren't ready to accept that *they* were killing the patients.

With a lot of coercing, cajoling and at a high personal cost, Semmelweis managed to convince his fellow practitioners and medical students to wash their hands with chlorinated solution between procedures. They obliged for a few months. And guess what? The mortality rate declined from 18.3 per cent in April 1847 to just 2.2 per cent by June 1847, and to near zero in the months to come. But what happened to Semmelweis? He was ridiculed, barred from practicing medicine, sent to an asylum, tortured and, days later, died. He paid the price of his life to save ours. Today, thankfully, handwash is institutionalized at all major medical centres around the world, and makes the greatest difference between life and death, notwithstanding the advances in medicines and surgeries.

The pain of the mothers disturbed Semmelweis so much that he admitted to life being worthless. That's deep heart for you. He painstakingly followed the doctors and medical students on their routines and isolated cadaverous particles as a possible cause. That's clear head. But consequentially, he put his career and eventually his life on the line to make his rather innocuous idea of a 'handwash' to be given a serious try. That's thick skin. How many of us are willing to face a ridicule, let alone skip a promotion, to make our ideas win? That's why innovation is rare. It calls for personal risk-taking (PS: the key operative here is not risk).

In fact, thick skin is the hallmark of scientists, inventors and artists alike.

After finishing his diploma from the Polytechnic Institute in Zurich (1896–1900), the twenty-one-year-old Einstein was frantically applying for a teaching post to all known universities across Europe. None were interested in hiring him. Out of despair, he reached out to schools and private tuitions but to little success. Finally, with the help of his friend and scientific collaborator, Marcel Grossmann, Einstein secured the job of a patent examiner level III at the Swiss Patent Office in Bern. That's where, after working for eight hours a day, six days a week, Einstein could manage to carry on his research on the sidelines, and published five papers in the Miracle Year of 1905. And guess what? Even with those credentials, nobody still hired him for a teaching role! That takes some thick skin, mutually.

As for the young Richard Feynman, 1939 wasn't the best year to graduate. After passing out from MIT, Feynman found it difficult to secure a summer job. For starters, it was the onset of the Second World War, and then nobody knew what to make of a physicist. It was not an in-demand talent. Even the famed Bell Labs would not look at this young graduate, though thanks to Bill Shockley, Feynman used to visit the place quite often. So, what did our man do? He joined his friend's chemicals company, where his job was to coat plastic and Bakelite with silver and make it look real.[31] The to-be Nobel laureate was quite okay blowing up a few test tubes at a forgettable place.

In fact, one of the driving philosophies of Feynman was *social irresponsibility*. In his memoir, *Surely You're Joking, Mr Feynman!*, the noted physicist credits this philosophy to the legendary mathematician John von Neumann. Feynman was told by von Neumann during his days at Los Alamos that 'You don't have to be responsible for the world that you're in.'[32] It's a radical thought, and quite against the grain.

So, here's a nudge for the creative class, courtesy Richard Feynman: 'You have no responsibility to live up to what other people think you ought to accomplish. I have no responsibility to be like they expect me to be. It's their mistake, not my failing.'[33]

That's quite a profound maxim to live by. And with pride, for you are unique.

Slow down, for it doesn't matter

Imagine you are a surgeon, and a good one at that. Which of the two propositions would you be more willing to operate with: a) it matters or b) it doesn't matter? The former translates strictly into 'the patient must survive', whereas the latter loosely reflects an ambivalence towards the outcome. What would you prefer? Most likely, the first one: it matters. And you are in the majority; after all, a surgeon puts you under the knife fully aware of the risk, including that of death. But can such a surgeon operate on her own child with that premise? I don't think so. She would be frozen if things deviate even slightly from the plan. She won't be able to improvise, for she has kept the end before the means. Most surgeons operate with the 'it doesn't matter' disposition.

It's hard to digest, right? Let us hear it from a surgeon. Paul Kalanithi, about whom we will know a lot more later, was one of the foremost neurosurgeons in the world. 'We have assumed an onerous yoke, that of *mortal responsibility*,' writes Kalanithi. 'Our patients' lives and identities may be in our hands, yet death always wins. Even if you are perfect, the world isn't. The secret is to know that the deck is stacked, that you will lose, that your hands or judgement will slip, and yet still struggle to win for your patients. You can't ever reach perfection, but you can believe in an asymptote toward which you are ceaselessly striving.'[34] Know that the deck is stacked! And yet you must strive.

When I advocate the position of 'it doesn't matter', I am not suggesting that you don't care; rather that you care only about what you can do to the best of your abilities and being fully aware that you just can't control the outcome. 'It doesn't matter' underscores the fleetingness of every moment, every emotion, the whole life.

'Real generosity toward the future lies in giving all to the present,' notes the Nobel laureate in literature, Albert Camus. You must learn to *surrender* to the outcome, surrender to the universal intelligence. 'It doesn't matter' can be a hugely liberating thought, one which lets you be completely soaked into the process so that you have no mental faculty left to worry about the outcome. You must plan but you can't be enslaved by the plan.

Writes Khalil Gibran:[35]

Your joy is your sorrow unmasked.
And the selfsame well from which your laughter rises was oftentimes filled with your tears.
And how else can it be?
The deeper that sorrow carves into your being, the more joy you can contain.

Because if you take a stance that it matters and that it *must* matter, then you are being rigid, setting up a conflict between yourself and the course of nature—not being one with nature. This avoidable resistance, as we will discuss in greater detail, is the very seed of suffering. Notes His Holiness the Dalai Lama, 'Denial of impermanence represents one of the main causes of suffering in our existences.'[36] If we understand the impermanency of the world and of all its components, the pertinent question is: Why harbour permanent emotions about temporary stuff?

When asked about his life's secret, the spiritual guru Jiddu Krishnamurti is said to have noted, 'I don't mind what happens.' It doesn't mean I don't *care* what happens, it's just that I *accept* whatever happens.

Let me share a personal experience on this theme. When I get into a conversation with a client, I can possibly operate from two paradigms: 1) I must win the deal, or 2) It doesn't matter even if I don't win the deal. Which one is the right attitude? In my twenties, I took the approach of 'must win', whereas in the thirties, I embraced the latter option. How does it help? Tremendously, I would say. If I get into a conversation with a perspective that I must win, I end up giving away more than I should. I tend to bend over backwards to meet the rather idiosyncratic demands of the client, which may not be good for me in the medium or long run, let alone for them. But if I operate with the slant that it's okay to lose this customer, I would be honest to myself and sincere to my profession. After all, there must be self-selection in every avenue. (PS: If I start losing too many customers, then it's time to introspect).

Recently, a learning and development professional reached out to me with a request for a design thinking workshop for her company. I shared a proposal and took her through it, but she asked, 'Can we do it with a larger batch size and in an online format?' I told her that sure we could, but the learning would suffer. After some back and forth, she remained steadfast on her demands. So, finally, I asked, 'Are you really interested in learning for your folks or is it just a tick-mark exercise?' To her credit, she admitted that yes, it was a tick-mark exercise. The workshop never transpired. I have saved a lot of time and effort and gained peace of mind by surrendering to the larger, universal intelligence and not being adamant that everything I touch should turn into gold.

The core philosophy of 'it doesn't matter' is surrendering to nature, to the will of nature. It's not that you should not do your best; rather, you should surrender *after* you have done your part and not before. It's the awareness that beyond your intellect, there exists a universal intelligence, which is ancient, pervasive and superior. It's just that you need to trust that universal intelligence. Ultimately all things are small, as all things are impermanent. Then why so serious?

The only thing that ultimately matters, says Eckhart Tolle, is this:[37]

Can I sense my essential Beingness, the I Am, in the background of my life at all times? To be more accurate, can I sense the I Am that I Am at this moment? Can I sense my essential identity as consciousness itself? Or am I losing myself in what happens, losing myself in the mind, in the world?

This perspective can set in only if you deliberately choose to slow down.

It takes time to be able to soak yourself into what is consequential in the long run. Everything looks urgent and even important, now. In a world of big data and cold statistics, what matters is weak signals and warm whispers, often internal. In a very incisive tone, Roger Federer talks about the perils of speed and the importance of slowing down: 'We're living in a very statistic-based world. We love our statistics, and we love breaking records . . . You just won a grand slam, or you're just world number one . . . Instead of enjoying it, we have to move on too quickly.'[38] Remember, Federer belongs to a sport that gets punishing the older you get, and yet he is comfortable slowing down!

Frankly, if you don't learn to enjoy your present moment, the results will always cheat you, for you are perpetually parking all joy for the next moment. The master of slowing down in the corporate world is Jeff Bezos. He is so good at seeking diverse views on important decisions that he jokingly calls himself Amazon's 'Chief Slowdown Officer'. He laments, 'I ask the team that I want to see this one more way and the teams working on it roll their eyes. I've already seen it 18 ways, but I thought of a 19th way and I want to see if that's correct for a high consequence irreversible decision.'[39] He involves himself only in high stake decisions and takes his time—sometimes making just three decisions a day, but ensuring that these are of highest quality. His life's mantra: *slow is smooth and smooth is fast.*

How has the attitude of going slow helped me on this book project? A lot, really. I have a certain cut-off date proposed by my publisher, and I need to work backwards. Suppose I decide a target to write 500 words per day, and further, that I must write during the morning hours or late night hours, or over the weekends to keep up with the target. What will happen if I missed these numbers? I will certainly feel miserable. Will the quality suffer? Of course.

Further, I must run my consulting business and honour my teaching responsibilities alongside this long writing journey. The key operative here is 'journey'. As long as I am at it, it doesn't matter how much I walk every day. What's important is the direction and that I keep walking. If I write, given every single opportunity, or research for my writing, I am being honest to my objectives. I have written pieces of this book at airport lounges, client offices, hotels, parks, cafes, flights, restaurants, schools and colleges, and not all of it at my desk at home. There are demands from family, self, clients and some unforeseen situations, but while playing my 'role' on all those fronts, if I keep coming back to writing this book, I won't be alarmed. After all, nobody will ever bother about how long I took to write this book—whether it's a dud or a bestseller.

Next, we talk about how we hone skills which keep us relevant today and in the future.

2

Deserve before Your Desire

'It did not really matter what we expected from life,
but rather what life expected from us.'

—Viktor Frankl[1]

At the time of writing this book, the generative artificial intelligence (AI) is threatening to take away the jobs of employees who are reluctantly returning to their offices after the long pandemic-enforced hiatus. The big question on everyone's mind is: 'Is my job secure, and, if so, for how long?'

This question was equally relevant in the England of the early 1800s, where the newly invented steam-powered looms were pushing textile workers into irrelevance. These 'Luddites' took on themselves the ominous task of saving mankind from the invasion of machines. How? By burning the machines down. Today's reaction isn't much better evolved either.

Ergo, the human reaction to the human-created technological advancement is neither new nor surprising. If the question is how technology is going to impact our life and career, I won't bother crystal gazing into the future. Rather,

I will draw insights and inspirations from the past. For the question has already been answered, except that we don't choose to see the writing on the wall.

'Technology isn't bad,' notes the historian Yuval Noah Harari. 'If you know what you want in life, technology can help you get it. But if you don't know what you want in life, it will be all too easy for technology to shape your aims for you and take control of your life.'[2] Take for instance the agriculture technology, which made a handful of people rich at the cost of millions toiling across the fields for less than desirable pays. Technology has its own knack of creating classes. The choice is yours.

The man-machine duet has a long and colourful past. Let's explore this in detail.

Use a machine without being one

The earliest known technologies were aimed at reducing human labour. Whether it be your humble wheel, or the more advanced pullies that were used to make the Egyptian pyramids, labour saving tools were the first form of technologies we encountered. Many of these we use on a day-to-day basis today, but we don't necessarily identify them as technologies anymore.

Now answer this—Who is physically stronger: you or your father, when of the same age? If I do an age-to-age comparison of you, your father and his father, you will quickly conclude that, at the age of thirty, your grandfather was probably stronger than your father and, certainly, you. And if I take this argument back a few generations, you wouldn't be far from concluding that we have grown weaker, physically. Our local environment doesn't demand that kind of physical labour and alas, what we don't use, we lose. And that's why gyms were invented. We need physical indulgence to remain vital.

So, here's what I propose:

Conjecture #1: Whenever machines get stronger, we humans get weaker.

Now that you understand that you might well be passing on a physically weaker gene, let's look at what else you have lost. Do you recollect your school or college days where you would comfortably remember over a dozen phone numbers and birth dates? Effortlessly, you would dial those numbers, surprising people and even yourself with your well-kept memory. Fast forward to today. How many phone numbers do you remember? Thanks to the OTPs (one-time passwords), the burden of remembering even your well-conjured passwords is eased out. The interesting thing is that it's not as if you don't have to remember, but that you *can't*. You store it to forget it, and technology is a good excuse. You use Google Maps to navigate the most familiar paths, so much so that you get stranded when the network is down, or when your phone misbehaves. You are enslaved by the mood swings of technology around you.

Which brings me to this:

Conjecture #2: Technology is a good slave, but a bad master.

I hope you 'remember' this.

Now that you understand how you have comprehensively lost your physical strength and the capacity to retrieve and recollect, let's look at the next victim. And this one is dearly human: our cognitive abilities. The *sapiens* of homo sapiens is under threat. There was a time when you would jump at 23 x 42 kind of arithmetic, and now you shiver looking at 1023 + 2059 kind of questions. From the humble calculators to the more sophisticated algorithms operating in the backdrop, you have lost out on your thinking abilities. Thanks to the revolution in computation and communication over the last few decades, you have systematically lost your natural intelligence in favour of artificial intelligence. What remains is natural stupidity.

Our physical incapacitation led to overreliance and exploitation of memory which, when taken away, led to us being more intelligence-focused and even this is now eased out of us, very much by our own doing. Figure 4 depicts the transition.

But as Eckhart so succinctly puts it, 'Thinking without awareness *is* the main dilemma of human existence.'[3] We mistakenly think that thinking is awareness. Technological advancements prompt us to take up higher order capabilities, but developing such capabilities isn't natural.

So, it seems:

Conjecture #3: Each new technology pushes you up the value chain.

The big question then is: what next? Which human ability is next in line for machine assault? Not so much an assault as much as competition of scarce resources between carbon and silicon. It may not be that much of a fight as much a banal surrender.

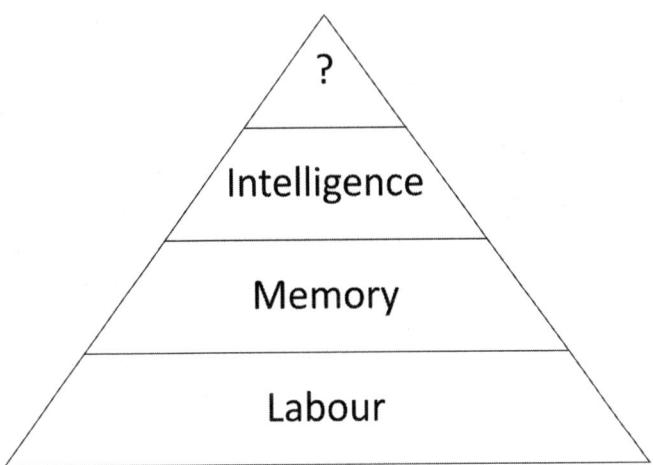

Figure 4: How technology has replaced our abilities, and what's next.

In the face of unprecedented advancements in biotech and infotech, an assemblage of machines will supersede a group of humans in almost any task. But the more difficult one to obliterate would be the individual human. 'Jobs that require specialization in a narrow range of routinised activities will be automated,' predicts Harari. 'But it will be much more difficult to replace humans with machines in less routine jobs that demand the simultaneous use of a wide range of skills, and that involves dealing with unforeseen scenarios.'[4] Does your job characterize such a scenario?

So, if you derive your prestige and relevance from working in groups or commanding a herd of humans, or even on ultra-specific areas with high levels of repeatability and certainty, you will be among the first ones to be knocked off by the intelligent machines. However, if you are more of an individual contributor, in science or arts, you will remain relevant for longer. You have to be either a specialist on a relevant topic or a person with a wide range, both cultivated painstakingly.

A case in point is the game of chess. For long, chess was considered as the epitome of human intelligence, never to be cornered by machines. And then it all broke down in 1997, the year IBM's Deep Blue took on the grandmaster Garry Kasparov and changed our beliefs for ever. On losing the sixth and final game of the match after just nineteen moves, the thirty-four-year-old Kasparov admitted, 'I lost my fighting spirit.'[5] Was it a prophecy on behalf of mankind?

Did we humans stop playing chess fearing that there's no point in competing with machines any longer? Rather, the exact opposite. Chess became a global sport, for now I can be matched with another player from another part of the world by a machine algorithm, and in return I get my international score. Thanks to platforms like www.chess.com, I can now (and I do) play any time, hone my skills, and never get predictable. Consequently, as of January 2023, India stands third, after Russia and China, on the list of grandmasters: an envious seventy-nine, of which twenty-seven have come in the past five years.[6] That's how machines up the game. Not by competing with us but by collaborating with us. But chess you still must master.

However, in the world of chess again, data can take you only thus far. With extremely powerful algorithms and engines that can endlessly analyse your every move, the onus of performance goes back to the player. 'If you simply look at a whole lot of variations without seeing a broader pattern or don't develop a fundamental understanding of what is happening in the larger landscape, then the data could be a burden rather than an aid,' admits the grandmaster Viswanathan Anand. [7] So, the premium goes back to the human.

The real draw of AI is to free up our time to do the more important stuff in life. As Google's former chief Eric Schmidt opines, 'We can build a future where AI-powered tools will both save us from mindless and time-consuming labour and also lead us to creative inventions and discoveries, encouraging breakthroughs that would otherwise take decades.' [8] However, this transition is nothing but natural, for the same AI continues to create newer ways to keep us numbly occupied.

This brings us back to the core question: What will remain sacrosanct to humans in the mid run? (I will leave the long run to the economists.)

I propose that there are three human virtues which we must protect for us to remain relevant: attention, empathy and creativity.

Attention is the starting point. Relaxed but alert attention. It's your ability to be in the present moment, instead of getting lost in the stream of internal or external chatter. 'Attention is not the same thing as concentration,' clarified Jiddu Krishnamurti. 'Concentration is exclusion; attention, which is total awareness, excludes nothing . . . And you can give your whole attention only when you care, which means that you really love to understand—then you give your whole heart and mind to find out.' [9] Attention seeks nothing, leaves nothing. It's just there, in the background, like a canvas, on which you can create. And you can already perceive how technology, especially social media and short videos, are butchering your attention with a thousand cuts. A simple piece of advice from Eckhart Tolle: 'Make sure the present moment is your friend, not your enemy.'[10]

Next comes empathy—your ability to understand others' stated and unstated thoughts and emotions. While machines have become intelligent, emotional intelligence remains the preserve of humans. But not all humans. Empathy is a skill that requires constant nurturing, for it's very easy to get lost in your own train of thought and assume what's good for others. Often, expertise comes at the cost of empathy—the more you know, the less you think others do. It's rare to have a subject matter expertise coupled with a wide range of rich emotions. Mastery comes with narrowing down one's aperture, saying 'no' to a thousand things, and going deep into a narrow allay—all counter to empathy, which calls for a range. As somebody wise once noted: 'People don't care how much you know until they know how much you care.'[11]

If empathy is about understanding problems, creativity is about solving problems. If intelligence deals with identifying, replicating and predicting patterns, creativity entails breaking patterns and forming newer ones. And as you realize, breaking patterns is anything but easy. So, if you have to remain relevant in the face of technological incursion, you must be willing to overcome a patterned way of thinking, and be comfortable with ambiguity.

The world of chess has some instructive insights to offer here. Chess grandmasters aren't better than average people when it comes to memory, as discovered by Dutch psychologist and chess player Adriaan de Groot. It's their ability to remember pieces in groups or patterns rather than individual pieces that offers them the edge. This chunking of memory, or more specifically, contextual memory, can serve you well till a stage. But thereafter you must learn to break away from your patterns and surprise the opponent. That's what India's Viswanathan Anand did with his famous 1.d4 opening (queen's pawn opening) against Vladimir Kramnik in the 2008 World Championship held at Bonn. Anand was always a 1.e4 (king's pawn opening) player. But by then his moves were thoroughly studied.[12] So, reinventing oneself is the only resort. But never an easy task at the highest levels of competition.

In fact, one of the real draws of creativity is that it makes you better at handling disorder. And because life, increasingly so, exposes you to its vagaries and uncertainties, you need to be creative to embrace it all. 'To live is to express oneself freely in creation,' said the artist-philosopher Bruce Lee.[13]

Remember Ignaz Semmelweis, the doctor who taught us the importance of a handwash? He died an isolated death at the hands of his own medical fraternity for proposing a preposterous idea—'What if the doctors are contaminating the patients?' You may think that over the years the medical fraternity has grown more scientific-minded and tolerant to being corrected, let alone challenged. Nothing is farther from the truth. If anything, today the third biggest cause of death in the US, after heart diseases and cancer, is medical errors.[14] In places like India, the story is the same, except we are not so rigorous with our data and forthright with our findings. Isn't it alarming that you get killed at the very place you visit to get better?

How do you arrest this? By bringing in more technology? Not really. In comes Peter Pronovost, a critical care specialist at the Johns Hopkins Hospital. He identified 'central line infections' at the ICUs as the major cause of death. And what was his proposal? A checklist. No fancy technology, but a list of to-dos on a simple sheet. If only doctors and nurses follow these simple protocols carefully, they could cut down deaths by almost half. In the state of Michigan alone, Pronovost's intensive care checklist protocol adopted over an eighteen-month period saved 1,500 lives and $100 million.[15] Imagine replicating this simple procedure across all major hospitals in your country. In fact, that's precisely how they keep your flights safe and prevent colossal buildings from falling. Checklists.

Atul Gawande, the MacArthur Fellow and one of the world's foremost surgeons, builds a strong case for how checklists are highly effective in scenarios ranging from construction sites to rescue operations, from aircraft cockpits to Michelin star restaurants and supermarkets. 'In the face of an extraordinarily complex problem, power needed to be pushed out of the center as far as possible,' notes Gawande. 'People need room to act and adapt . . . and they had learned to codify that understanding into simple checklists . . . The checklist gets the dumb stuff out of the way, the routines your brain shouldn't have to occupy itself with . . . and lets it rise above to focus on the hard stuff.'[16] These checklists are far more effective in saving lives than any technology. If anything, in medical science, technology is known to add more complications, apart from being prohibitively costly for the patients. (Think of the cost of da Vinci surgical systems vis-à-vis their benefits.)

Around the year 2007, Gawande worked with medical professionals and officers at the WHO to design a simple two-minute, nineteen-step surgery checklist to be rolled out at select hospitals to assess its effectiveness. They picked eight hospitals, one each in the US, Canada, UK, New Zealand, Philippines, Jordan, Tanzania and India. Just in three months of adoption of the checklist by the trained surgery teams, the rate of major complications fell by 36 per cent, and death came down by 47 per cent.[17] Notwithstanding the differences in skills, training, expertise, facilities and funding across these countries, the checklist did work. The best of the hospitals in the US or UK did gain as much as those in Tanzania.

A good checklist is where humans beat machines—it is simple, cheap, effective and transmissible. It starts with paying *attention* to the most crucial aspects of any problem. Then *empathizing* with the cognitive load that the actors might experience during such high-stake engagements, such as medical procedures or working on-board ISS (International Space Station). Finally, being *creative* to devise a list that is both simple and easy to comply. We can keep ourselves relevant, provided we acknowledge and preserve our differentiators, both individually and collectively as a species.

Now that you understand that your continued relevance hinges on how well you direct your attention towards honing empathy and creativity, let's look at some of the practical approaches.

Pay attention to your attention

Here is a sight at 5 a.m. at the Bengaluru International Airport: crowded, disciplined, but almost everybody glued to their screens—laptops, mobile phones or games. A rare sight of somebody catching up on sleep, or reading a newspaper or, in a rare case, a book. What's happening here? These are the people who are pretty much running our economy, and since

I am talking of Bengaluru, I can safely identify them driving the information age in this attention economy. But how about their attention? Short videos? Facebook? Instagram? Netflix? It's time to introspect.

Technology is a double-edged sword. While it frees up quite a bit of our time which would otherwise be involved in doing repetitive, low IQ tasks, the same technology throws at us myriad avenues of keeping ourselves distracted and meaninglessly occupied. Some may doubt if at all technology ever meant to save us time.

In 1981, at a public seminar at Brockwood Park, UK, Krishnamurti asked, 'When the machine can take over all the activities of the brain, then what happens to the brain?' He suggested two possibilities: either the brain pursues entertainment, or it pursues the inward processes of self-discovery. He warned that the entertainment industry is already gaining (remember, its 1981), and that there are very few who are concerned about the psychological understanding of man. He challenged us to truly go beyond the self, the ego, the bodily—towards internal discovery.[18] Forty years on, the entertainment industry, starring Meta, Netflix, Disney and IPL, has already won, and we are still not sure of what to make of all our intellectual and emotional capacities. If that doesn't worry you, it concerns me.

When I was growing up, I was constantly reminded that time is money and knowledge is power. As I come to realize it now, time is *not* money and knowledge is *not* power. Rather, *attention* is money, and the *application* of knowledge is power. And please don't confuse time with attention. Just because you are spending your time doing something, it doesn't mean you are paying your attention to it. How many times have you spotted yourself talking over the phone, fiddling with it, listening to a podcast, or even drafting a message, right in the middle of driving your car? Or rather, how often do you not engage in such acts? While your time is spent driving, your attention is elsewhere. Since driving doesn't take all your cognitive capacity, the surplus still needs some outlet and your mind discovers clever uses for itself, till you hit a divider, or worse, another being.

We are losing our attention to trivial stuff. We think we are getting high quality content, like news, songs, movies, lectures, games, funny cat videos, or even the insidious stuff, for free. Why not gobble it all up till the scheme lasts? But what we don't realize is that while the content is free, our attention is not. These companies are preying on our attention. Imagine what happens when your network is down, or you are stranded without your beloved phone? Do you feel relieved or miserable? I guess, you don't even want to think of such an eventuality. Little doubt, Facebook is the new cigarette, and a socially accepted one, without much of an age restriction. (PS: Facebook is a metaphor here.)

Tell me honestly how do you feel after having watched short videos or the ilk for a solid ten minutes—insightful, relieved, elated, thrilled, informed, energized? Or, guilty? I guess, it's a heavy guilt of having wasted your time, mindlessly. And, alas, this guilt lasts for only two minutes before the cycle starts all over again, lest people around nudge you out of it. For the brain, it's nicotine or a drug all over again. The brain can't differentiate. Your intellect can't. But your intelligence can. Your consciousness can. And that's what I am appealing to here.

I am not at all suggesting that you banish your social media life, for even I am a consumer of YouTube, Facebook,

LinkedIn and, occasionally, watch a movie or two on the OTT platforms. But I try to do it consciously, in my full awareness that I am doing so. It gets out of hand when you are no longer in control of your behaviour. And that could even be with your good old television set late in the night. Why blame mobile phones? At any rate, when you are not controlling your mind but rather are under complete control of your mind, it's a travesty. It could be alcohol, cigarettes, television, a loved one, a novel, a movie, cricket match, or short videos. When you are not alert while carrying out any act, it is an act of lack of consciousness, even though you may be fully awake during the act. Here, consciousness is not the same as consciousness in the clinical sense. It's alert awareness.

This alert awareness is mindfulness. The Vietnamese monk Thich Nhat Hanh defines mindfulness as the ability to 'keep your attention focused on the work, be alert and ready to handle ably and intelligently any situation which may arise.' Mindfulness is the 'miracle which can call back in a flash our dispersed mind and restore it to wholeness so that we can live each minute of life.'[19] It's not the absence of thinking or feeling, but its very awareness. Not to judge that you are right or wrong, but to be conscious of it. To acknowledge it.

In my profession of teaching and coaching, attention is everything. Unless I am fully attentive to what I am doing and my audience is fully into it, there can't be any exchange of knowledge, let alone ideas. So, I must ensure that there is attention. How? Firstly, by cutting down on all distractions. In my workshops, no participant is allowed to carry a mobile phone or a laptop. All mobile phones are either kept in a carton box or in respective bags. Laptops are closed, including mine. Secondly, I try to keep the content rich and approach unpredictable. Since I don't use presentations for my sessions, there's no obligation for me to finish something pre-meditated and neither does my audience know what's coming up. Both the parties are exploring the turf and that uncertainty keeps everyone alert.

Thirdly, I give the practice first and then the theory. Instead of relaying a concept and then asking the participants to follow it, they first practise the concept, experience its utility first-hand and then I share what it's called and the theory behind it. It stays. No point in teaching anything that doesn't work, especially in executive education or corporate training programmes. If your audience doesn't pay attention to what you are saying, it's your problem and not theirs. And it's your responsibility, and not theirs, that they pay attention. Do whatever it takes, including the temporarily distasteful edicts.

How to bring more attention to your life? I can answer from two perspectives: a few practices and a fundamental rule. Let's start with the rule. The key rule is to not let your brain control you. And the most suitable tool is meditation. In simpler terms, meditation is the gateway to being present in the moment, instead of regretting the past or contemplating the future. In principle, meditation is a method of direct observation of one's own mind. It's a means of keeping your mind where your body is, which is seldom the case. As per Krishnamurti, 'Meditation is a state of mind which looks at everything with complete attention, totally, not just parts of it.'[20]

Ray Dalio, the co-chairman and founder of Bridgewater Associates, and one of the most accomplished investors in the world, has been practising transcendental meditation since

1960s. He was introduced to this style of meditation by the music band. The Beatles and his exposure to India. Dalio claims that every big success in his life is attributed to meditation.[21] That's a very big endorsement, indeed.

Yuval Harari is big on Vipassana meditation, a technique that involves sixty days of silent retreat here in India. The historian claims that meditation has helped him enhance focus and to distinguish between what's real and the story created by the mind. 'For me, not just in meditation, but when I work, I try to be very, very disciplined with my attention not to allow external forces to take control of my attention,' claims Harari.[22] He attributes his entire work, including the landmarks *Sapiens* and *Homo Deus,* to meditation.

Here's a little surprise for you.

'I came to the conclusion that really we should aspire to increase the scope and scale of human consciousness in order to better understand what questions to ask,' says Elon Musk. 'The only thing that makes sense to do is strive for greater collective enlightenment.' Now, you don't expect Musk to talk about enlightenment. Do you? And yet that's how he not only maintains an enormous knowledge differential, but also the pursuit of innovation. As anyone who has worked alongside Musk would attest, the man is deeply spiritual about his outlook and meditative about his work.

It doesn't require any special practice like deep breathing exercises, chanting, concentrating on anything in particular or not focusing on anything at all. All it takes is to be present, fully. Reading this book with full attention is meditation. Being totally involved in whatever you are doing is meditative, and yet being aware that you are doing it consciously and that you can get out of it at your will (which doesn't happen in the middle of an online game or a movie).

In terms of practices, here's what has helped me enormously:

- Turn off all notifications. You, and not others, decide when you want to get interrupted.
- Exit as many WhatsApp or Telegram groups as you possibly can. Many won't even notice your absence.
- Keep your phone on silent mode. And away from you, at home. Much like the old landline phones. Picking it up should take some effort.
- Never attend a meeting where you don't make or get a significant value add. At least don't attend a meeting out of fear.
- Avoid small talk. Small talk mostly remains small.
- Never ever travel without a book. Even locally.
- Spend 0.5 per cent of your monthly salary on buying physical books. You don't remember much while reading online or listening to audio books.
- Read ten pages of something/anything in a physical format before sleeping. It will show up remarkably after a few years.
- Be very selective about people you spend time with. Silence is great company.
- In conferences, or large gatherings, focus on having one or two deep, meaningful conversations rather than a hundred exchanges of cards. No one remembers your card; they remember you.
- Avoid using presentations. Personify the content and speak from your heart. People will love you for that.

- Have dedicated thinking time per day, per week. Ideally thirty to sixty minutes per day, where you are thinking about non-operational, non-urgent issues.

Let me bring your attention to the topic of reading books. What's the best way to read a book with the intent of remembering and applying the learning: physical, e-book or an audio version? I believe that real learning is visceral and not just conceptual. If you learn about problem-solving and take copious notes and yet fail to apply them in a real-life situation, then it doesn't matter what you have learnt. In fact, you haven't learnt it unless it's in your veins. With that intent, if you wish to learn something useful and be able to apply it, I recommend reading a physical book.

John Medina, a developmental molecular biologist and the author of *Brain Rules*, argues that information is remembered best when it is elaborate, meaningful and contextual. Further, the greater number of handles you create at the moment of learning, the more likely you are to remember it later.[23] When you read a book, not only are more of your senses involved (sight, touch, smell, taste and even hearing), but you are also viscerally involved. You scribble on the margins, make your own notes, underline the important stuff, paraphrase the concepts, revisit and revise. This multimodal reinforcement greatly enhances memory of what you read. Also, it is well established that repetition over spaced intervals helps in learning. Since books stare at you from your shelves, you are more likely to pick those than the e-books hidden in your devices.

In contrast, when you are listening to an audio book, you are almost always doing it in parallel with something else, like driving a car, and hence while you may think you are learning, you are getting entertained, at best. Your attention and retention both suffer. (Try writing down key takeaways of what you were listening to while driving last week.) Moreover, you can read two or three times faster than you can listen, as you can skip words while reading but can't while listening. Similarly, with reading e-books you don't get to interact with the book in a way that your mind has evolved over the eons to grasp concepts. Electronic mediums severely limit the number of senses involved while making sense of the world around you. That's perhaps why virtual reality or augmented reality doesn't pose a threat to the tourism industry.

I have three Kindles at home and over 1000 physical books. I rarely use Kindle, let alone Audible. I may be an exception, but the practice of reading physical books has served me well. The choice of reading format is very much personal, but if you pay attention to how you conserve and converge your attention, you are good for the next rungs: empathy and creativity.

Practise compassion and be empathetic

In the pursuit of making machines more like humans, we humans are becoming more like machines. So, if you pride yourself on being super productive, great at multi-tasking, knowing it all, and being omnipresent, if not omnipotent, you know exactly whom you are aping. The call is to retain the humanity in us humans.

Evolutionary biologists allege that one of the defining characteristics of our species is symbolic reasoning. For instance, if you see a colleague upset about something, it doesn't take you long to figure out the possible reasons, and to relate it to what happened in the recent past. 'She's upset because she didn't get to be on that important project'—that's your symbolic reasoning at play. It's highly intuitive and quite innate in us. This forms what psychologists call the 'Theory of Mind'—our capacity to understand other people's intentions and motivations by ascribing mental states to them. Somebody is upset, delighted, afraid, irritated, nervous, elated and any of that, by a mere tone of voice. We are not only predicting others' mental state but are also moved (read emote) to act appropriately. Empathy is an innate property, but with varying degrees of development, and so is compassion.

So, let's delve deeper on how to be genuinely empathetic.

Harvard's Daniel Goleman, a renowned researcher on emotional intelligence, describes empathy as 'the ability to understand the emotional makeup of other people', and the 'skill in treating people according to their emotional reaction.'[24] It is clear that empathy starts with understanding your own emotional state. Once you are aware of how you are feeling and are, hopefully, in control of it, only then do you have the cognitive and affective capacity to understand others.

But read Goleman's definition once again, carefully. Do you think machines have yet evolved to 'understand' people's emotional makeup and 'treat' them as per their emotional reactions? Not yet. And I don't see that as a real threat in the near future. Because any such attempt from a machine, whether taught by humans or self-taught, won't come across as authentic. And you, from a very early age, have a very acute ability to make out what's not authentic. You can fool a child with a fake toy, but not fake joy. It's almost natural to us.

So, we have a neat advantage here. But not everyone is equally in the lead.

Empathy emerges from compassion. 'Compassion, what I sometimes also call human *affection*, is the determining factor of our life,' says His Holiness the Dalai Lama. 'Connected to the palm of the hand, the five fingers become functional; cut off from it, they are useless. Similarly, every human action becomes dangerous when it is deprived of human feeling. When they are performed with feeling and respect for human values, all activities become constructive.'[25] And compassion and empathy are far from technology.

Empathy and compassion have a wide range of impact, from core spirituality to hard economics. And yet emotions are often considered a sign of weakness, of indecisiveness. Being emotional often gets a bad rap, for business seems to be devoid of such nebulous issues, but if anything, being emotionally intelligent is core to leadership and innovation. As the celebrated leadership coach, Marshall Goldsmith, says, 'One of the most important qualities of living an earned life is building positive relationships . . . We can all admit that empathy is one of the most important variables in building relationships.'[26] Yet, in most promotion or hiring interviews, EQ (empathy quotient) takes a backseat. The focus is mostly on relevant work experience and 'in-season' skills.

I don't consider myself terribly empathetic, and those who know me wouldn't be surprised by this assertion. However, I discovered the 'empathy switch' in my mind the day I became a father. Suddenly, I was dealing with a fellow human who couldn't communicate in a manner I was used to. What I was holding on to was extremely fragile, and yet helplessly adorable. And that day onwards, I have become increasingly empathetic, in personal life and at work. We tend to limit empathy to special occasions, but as Microsoft CEO Satya Nadella reminds us, empathy is not what you reserve only for your family or friends, but also for your customers and employees.[27] And that is the brand of empathy that I am interested in here: empathy in the professional realm.

We generally tend to swing between empathy and apathy in most business or business-like conversations. Tuning in to a high-profile customer, we tend to listen a lot better and interrupt a lot less, while in the same breath, we don't mind cutting off a colleague mid-sentence. Our empathy is finely calibrated. In certain milieus, like in a customer care centre, we come across as naturally caring and listening, whereas during appraisals it's not hard to see us stonewalling emotions. But regardless, being empathetic is going to be even more critical, for most low-end jobs will be cornered by machines, and we will be increasingly pushed towards self-discovery and renewal.

Here are three tips on being more empathetic towards people in a professional context, without being asked or paid for demonstrating such behaviours. Firstly, *listen with intent*, not just to the words but the meaning behind them, keeping the speaker, and not you, in the spotlight. Secondly, *observe with purpose*. Attend to the body language, the unstated, the eyes, the hand movements, the context, what transpired and what's coming up. Lastly, *defer judgement*, for your judgement rarely serves you well. This primordial instinct certainly leaves you more embarrassed than enlightened on most occasions. Do you remember the last time you judged a newly minted team member, slotting her in one of the camps, just to discover how much of learning you missed out on? Work by Julian Treasure, William Ury, David Phillips and Kate Murphy, among others, will be very handy in sharpening your listening skills and overall empathy.

Think about the four core communication means: reading, writing, speaking and listening. Reading and listening are inputs, while speaking and writing are outputs. Now, answer this: How will you stack these four in terms of usage on a daily basis? Let me hazard a guess: speaking, listening (not hearing), reading and writing. And if you realize that you are speaking and writing an awful lot more than you are reading or listening, know that you have not only gone predictable but also stale. You need to up your ante on quality listening and quality reading. Else, where's your fresh input coming from? Talking comes relatively easy, but listening and contemplating aren't that accessible. The core to empathy is being comfortable with your emotions and only then are others' emotions accessible to you.

Listening, which I believe is core to empathy, can be cultivated, or rather it must be. It's a surefire way of not only understanding others but also earning their trust. 'In modern life, we are encouraged to listen to our hearts, listen to our inner voices, and listen to our guts, but rarely are we encouraged to listen carefully and with intent to other people,' observes the journalist Kate Murphy. 'To really listen is to be moved physically, chemically, emotionally, and intellectually by another person's narrative.'[28]

Have you ever come across anyone at a party complaining, 'Avoid that person, he *listens* a lot!' Listens a lot? I will surely take that as a compliment. On the contrary, the most common accusation is that he speaks a lot, or that he doesn't ever listen.

So, if you wish to be the centre of the next gathering, try listening, genuinely and generously. The magnetic quality of good listeners can be summed up as 'inverse charisma'; they make you feel important.

As Khalil Gibran wrote: [29]

> You talk when you cease to be at peace with your thoughts;
> And when you can no longer dwell in the solitude of your heart you live in your lips, and sound is a diversion and a pastime.
> And in much of your talking, thinking is half murdered. For thought is a bird of space, that in a cage of words may indeed unfold its wings but cannot fly.

Next time you open your mouth to speak, just ask yourself: 'Is what I am about to say worth it?'

So much for empathy. But if left unchecked, it can also make you quite miserable. Let's understand how.

A case for bounded empathy

Is there a downside to empathy? Can it lead to emotional exhaustion? While it is important to know your emotional state and that of others, you must avoid situations where, in an attempt to making others happy, you end up making yourself miserable. It's not all that uncommon.

If you find it difficult to say a 'high quality no' to your abusive supervisor, then it's not empathy but lack of courage and clarity. If you fail to arrest students moving in and out of the class during your lecture, that's not freedom but lack of discipline. If your colleagues don't respect your personal space and time, and always expect you to join them over a cup of tea, that's your lack of spine. If a company fails to discipline its customers under the misplaced pretext of customer centricity, it's bankruptcy. Never have a misplaced sense of empathy. This is what the person whom you're empathizing with is thinking: *Don't you dare feel sorry for me. I'm here to kill you.*

The trouble with excessive empathy is that not only does it plague your professional life, but it also manifests on the personal account. Take, for instance, your children. When should you give in to their demands and where should you draw the line, lest you end up giving up entirely? I have picked this sensitive topic to drive home the very point that empathy must be demonstrated within boundaries, or else it hurts all involved. The psychologist Jordan Peterson is a big proponent of disciplining children. In a rather bold fashion he offers, 'More often than not, modern parents are simply paralyzed by the fear that they will no longer be liked or even loved by their children if they chastise them for any reason. They want their children's friendship above all, and are willing to sacrifice respect to get it.'[30] That's hard hitting, indeed.

Sam Walton was famous for involving his children and extended family in almost all aspects of his business from the very early days. His children would be involved in buying, merchandising, surveying properties and, later, investing in Walmart. He treated them as adults, and they grew up to become good friends. That's how empathy is conditioned in the most private settings. In business, there is much less room for bouncing back from misplaced empathy. You might go belly-up by the time you realize it.

Containing your emotions, in general, and empathy, in particular, may be a daunting challenge in a personal milieu, but relatively a straightforward task on the professional front. Or so we think. But there are professions built on this exact practice of bounded empathy. The airlines industry is instructive in this regard.

Let's revisit a familiar scenario. You are rushing towards your boarding gate and have barely managed to get in before the twenty-five-minute gate closure cut-off. Then there are other travellers who aren't as swift or lucky. How does the ground staff react to them? While the staff is all smiles for you during the entire journey, their empathy ceases the moment you are even a minute late at the departure gate. You may cry, howl, blackmail or wield your contacts and power, the gate ain't opening. For such a time, empathy is reserved for those on the *other* side of the gate—the customers who are awaiting a timely take-off. It doesn't make business sense to demonstrate empathy to all, and under all circumstances. Ergo, empathy has a boundary condition. Unlike airlines where the scope of empathy is explicit, most everyday professional dealings leave a lot to guesswork. And that's where we have a case for bounded empathy, as shown in Figure 5.

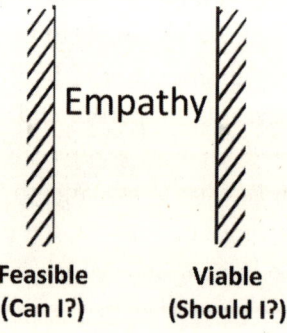

Figure 5: Empathy bounded by what's feasible and what's viable.

You exhibit empathy not in a boundless manner. Your good senses about others are bounded by what you can and what you should do. If your subordinate is slacking repeatedly on ordinary tasks and you fail to take a stern action, it's because of your misplaced sense of empathy which, to others, rightly smells of meekness. You must limit your emotions to what's good for business (viable) and what's practical (feasible).

In fact, one of the growing criticisms of design thinking is on account of its excessive focus on empathy, at the cost of expertise. The claim of the design thinking community is that you give us any problem and we can solve it by applying our standard processes and tools of design. But scores of unfinished projects and unkept promises have left the practitioners and their clients sober. In an *MIT Technology Review* article, writer and designer Rebecca Ackermann cites the case of San Francisco Unified School District where the ambitious School Food Advisory (SFA) project took its own shape after numerous interventions from the design consultancy IDEO. She notes, 'Nearly a decade after IDEO completed its work, the best results have been due to the expertise of the district's own team and its generations of students, not the empathy that went into the initial short-term consulting project.'[31] Empathy can't replace sheer expertise and the skills it takes to execute on time and budget. Or else, it's all feel-good, happy stuff.

In most design thinking workshops, the initial excitement around insight clinics, brainstorming sessions, mind maps, quick and dirty prototypes, et al., often doesn't amount to much that is robust or enduring. And it's because empathy is often considered as an end in itself. That's what Marshall Goldsmith warns leaders about: 'The most effective empathic gesture is the empathy of doing—when you go beyond understanding, feeling, and caring and actually take action to make a difference.'[32] You must, after all, act on your empathy. Consequently, empathy must give way to action, and this calls for certain boundary conditions.

Bounded empathy means you operate between possibilities, yet with a humanness. Not to over promise, not to undermine. As Paul Kalanithi recollects his encounters with dying patients, he reflects, 'Openness to human relationality does not mean revealing grand truths from the apse; it means meeting patients where they are, in the narthex or nave, and bringing them as far as you can.'[33] And yet they may die and you must move to the next case, with the same zeal. The practice of bounded empathy not only saves you from self-tormenting, but also shields others from emotional hysteresis, the highs and lows of your promises.

Let's now talk about what follows empathy: creation!

Create, don't manage. Actualize, don't intellectualize.

Humans are the agents of creation. We created the very AI and other technological tools that we are learning to fear. But as Yuval Noah Harari incisively offers: 'Humans were always far better at inventing tools than using them wisely.'[34] Creation is your ultimate antidote to obscurity. The real deal is to *create* a better version of yourself, not so much creating a clever contraption.

If you have reached thus far in the book, I might have managed to transfer my concepts of life and work to you and hopefully helped germinate some new ones. However, this book won't be of much help in practical terms if you don't take conscious efforts to translate what you know into what you do. To intellectualize or even to conceptualize is relatively easy; the hard thing is to actualize. As Bruce Lee would quip, 'You have that personal obligation to yourself to make yourself the best *product* possible according to your own terms. Not the *biggest* or the *most successful*, but the best quality—with that achieved, comes everything else.'[35] He would identify life's ultimate goal as to actualize oneself.

I believe that the premium in life is on creation, not so much the avoidance of ruin. Because the second law of thermodynamics will always win, for the entropy, or degree of randomness, will increase with time. You can channelize all your energies into maintaining and managing something of vitality, but you still will have to wait for a creative spark. Better to create, and let others manage it.

Who is the creator of Taj Mahal? Shah Jahan, of course. For almost 400 years now, that marvel of contemporary architecture and construction has been a magnet for tourists from around the world. But take a moment to consider that there is a team looking after the monument and they have a leadership structure and a hierarchy to talk about. Any idea who's the vice president of that team? Or the CEO? Nope. You don't know and, moreover, you don't care. That's the difference between creating and managing. No one remembers you for what you manage well, but for what you create.

And yet, scores of engineers (the word 'engineer' means to contrive or devise) are busy getting promoted as managers. Initially they created. Then they overlooked those who created. And then managed those who managed those who created, and ad infinitum to a point where they forgot creating. In the age of technology, the premium, surprisingly, will be on creation. Think of how much a manager acts between you and the Ola cab driver, or when you are buying stocks or other financial instruments at ICICI Direct. Technology erodes the middle layer.

On creating and how it is divine, Phil Knight, the founder of Nike, offers:[36]

> When you make something, when you improve something, when you deliver something, when you add some new thing or service to the lives of strangers, making them happier, or healthier, or safer, or better, and when you do it all crisply and efficiently, smartly, the way everything should be done but so seldom is—you're participating more fully in the whole grand human drama. More than simply alive, you're helping others to live more fully, and if that's business, all right, call me a businessman.

Most of entrepreneurship is creativity. We delve into entrepreneurs a little later in the book. For now, let's look at employees.

Is intelligence the same as creativity? Is every idea creative? Is creativity the same as innovation? No, to all.

As discussed before, intelligence builds patterns while creativity destroys patterns. I would rather call creativity as fluid intelligence—your ability to seamlessly connect dots across domains in hitherto unknown formations. Not every idea is creative, for only those ideas that are novel and useful qualify. Novelty is about newness to the context (and not to the world), whereas utility implies practicality and viability. A new idea that works is a creative one. And while creativity is the act of generating ideas, innovation is that of implementing ideas. Not surprisingly, very few ideas see the light of day, owing to several reasons, chief of which is intent. In short, you must learn to raise the bar of what qualifies as truly creative, let alone innovative.

As Henry Ford speaks of new ideas: 'It is better to be sceptical of all new ideas and to insist upon being shown rather than to rush around in a continuous brainstorm after every new idea.' Stating an often-overlooked truth, Ford clarifies that 'Ideas are of themselves extraordinarily valuable, but an idea is just an idea. Almost any one can think up an idea. The thing that counts is developing it into a practical product.'[37] The premium is in the execution.

Henry Ford gave shape to his automobile dream during the 1880s and 1890s, while working on engines at Westinghouse and, later, Edison Electric. His early experiments culminated into a Quadricycle which he launched in 1896, and for the vehicle he got an approval from his childhood hero Thomas Edison. In 1899, he started his first venture, Detroit Automobile Company, with the financial backing from Detroit lumber baron William H. Murphy. But soon, Murphy ran out of patience, and he pulled the plug in 1901. Ford's second enterprise launched soon after, Henry Ford Company, met with a similar fate, this time at the hands of the external managers Murphy brought in.

Two failures by the age of thirty-nine would have derailed most, but Ford persevered and, in 1902, with the backing of Alexander Malcomson, a coal magnate, Ford started the company that exists till date. The Ford Motor Company introduced the Model A in 1904, and his 1908 production of the Model T revolutionized manufacturing forever. Noted the father of the assembly line, 'Failure is simply the opportunity to begin again, this time more intelligently.'[38]

It's not for the want of a genius idea that most entrepreneurs or leaders alike perish. Success hinges on their ability to execute that idea. However, you must allow a few ideas to die. In fact, a lot of ideas must die, for you and your team must have the aptitude and perseverance to overcome the hurdle rate of creativity. It's like the theory of evolution applied to ideas and, fortunately, evolution requires that the risk of extinction be present. 'Our survival depended upon chaotic, reactive information-gathering experiences. That's why one of our best attributes is the ability to learn through a series of increasingly self-corrected ideas,' notes John Medina.[39]

Now that you are up to speed on the vocabulary of creativity, let's consider the more pressing problem: How to be creative. Three tips: 1) follow your curiosity but keep pivoting; 2) retain a fluid identity; and 3) protect your hobbies from your profession.

Since these are high density topics, let's delve into them at leisure. But before that, here is what one of the most creative types, Albert Einstein, had to offer: 'It is important to foster individuality, for only individuals can produce the new ideas.'[40] And you will find individuality the most difficult idea to accept!

Follow your curiosity, but keep pivoting

In a 1996 interview with *Wired* magazine, Steve Jobs, then heading NeXT, opined:[41]

> Creativity is just connecting things. When you ask creative people how they did something, they feel a little guilty

because they didn't really do it, they just saw something. It seemed obvious to them after a while. That's because they were able to connect experiences they've had and synthesize new things. And the reason they were able to do that was that they've had more experiences or they have thought more about their experiences than other people.

These are brilliant observations from a person who was still years shy of launching the iPod, iPhone and iPad, and, most importantly, the creativity renaissance at Apple.

In his 2018 letter to Amazon's shareholders, Bezos establishes the importance of wandering around:[42]

Sometimes (often actually) in business, you do know where you're going, and when you do, you can be efficient. Put in place a plan and execute. In contrast, wandering in business is not efficient . . . but it's also not random. It's guided—by hunch, gut, intuition, curiosity, and powered by a deep conviction that the prize for customers is big enough that it's worth being a little messy and tangential to find our way there. Wandering is an essential counterbalance to efficiency. You need to employ both.

As somebody who prizes the power of intuition, curiosity and wandering around more than data or luck, Bezos argues that creativity calls for the intersection of a deep domain expertise and a beginner's mind. He is quick to note, however, that once people achieve a certain level of expertise, they find it very hard to keep an open mind to the possibilities, and that's where creativity suffers.[43] Both Jobs and Bezos point towards one direction: curiosity. Curiosity beyond your favourite domain, your turf, your comfort zone. Curiosity is natural to us but to maintain it, alas, isn't.

To understand curiosity, we need to rewind our lives a bit.

Why do children ask so many questions? One is that they don't know much, for everything is new to them. Also, they want to explore the world around them, as much and as fast as possible. But more importantly, they don't have inhibitions. They aren't perturbed about what others, including the important others, will say or think about them. Fast forward to adulthood and, suddenly, the same child stops asking questions. It's not that she has grown more knowledgeable or less interested, but has evidently developed a heightened sense of inhibition.

There is no better path to creativity than curiosity. As the author Elizabeth Gilbert shares, 'I think that the difference between a tormented creative life and a tranquil creative life is nothing more than the difference between the word *awful* and the word *interesting*.'[44] If you fail to see things as interesting, including the distasteful but instructive experiences, you will, most likely, repel creativity.

As it turns out, while maintaining curiosity is difficult, even more daunting is the ability to pivot, to jettison what's not working. Learn to pivot if your curiosity leads you astray. Otherwise, most of your explorations will be fruitless, if not hazardous. If you are adventurous enough to explore things in life, be humble enough to also forgive yourself and courageous enough to move to the next expedition. Children are explorers by nature, but the adults around them create sufficient doubts in their minds that failure is fatal, and embarrassment is permanent. We need to rethink such notions as parents.

Chess grandmaster Viswanathan Anand classifies players into those with a horizontal approach and those who pursue a vertical path. Horizontal players are like a banyan tree with a broad understanding and an ability to respond to each stimulus and provocation differently. They are versatile and it makes them difficult to plan against. Vertical players go down straight paths, trekking deeper into variations and problem-solving, and are more akin to a palm tree.

Anand concedes that as the game evolves, the horizontal players remain relevant with their diversity and flexibility, and the fuel is their curiosity. 'Curiosity fuels your mind and spreads your knowledge base, which inevitably expands your repertoire, makes you flexible and agile, allows you to adapt and promptly respond to changing circumstances, and increases the chances of serendipity coming to your aid,' notes Anand. Little surprise, Anand is going strong even forty years after he first became a national champion.

Adam Grant, in his book *Think Again*, offers a strong case of rethinking your perspectives in life. 'A hallmark of wisdom is knowing when it's time to abandon some of your most treasured tools and some of the most cherished parts of your identity,' opines Grant. You have blind spots in your knowledge and opinions, which have been laboured through years of thinking and doing, but they can't take you any further. You must learn to pivot, which is anything but easy. Pivoting calls for 'confident humility'. Known for his ability to let go of the sunk cost fallacy, the Nobel laurate Daniel Kahneman confides, 'Being wrong is the only way I feel sure I've learned anything . . . My attachment to my ideas is provisional. There's no unconditional love for them.'[45] That's a great attitude to have. Creativity calls for curiosity, and it necessitates that you move from one failure to another, fast. It requires an experimental mindset.

Jeff Bezos identifies experimentation as the cornerstone of creativity, entrepreneurship and an innovative culture. While talking to officers of the US Air Force, the Amazon founder pointed out, 'You need to do more experiments per week per month per year per decade, it's that simple. You cannot invent without experimenting.'[46] He notes that if you know it's going to work in advance, it is not an experiment. And that you should not confuse experimentation with operational excellence. He persists that a few wildly successful experiments can pay for hundreds of failed ones. Productive experiments are long-tailed, they take care of a lot of failure elsewhere. So, not experimenting is costlier than experimenting.

As a case in point, Amazon failed with its Fire Phone, but the insights came in handy while developing ensuing products. As Bezos clarifies, 'Development of the Fire Phone and Echo was started around the same time. While the Fire Phone was a failure, we were able to take our learnings (as well as the developers') and accelerate our efforts building Echo and Alexa.'[47] Ditto for Google Glass. While the original innovation was a commercial failure, owing to several reasons, chiefly privacy and security, the technology gave shape to the promising Google Lens which is integrated to the Android OS based phones.[48]

At Microsoft, the search engine Bing didn't turn out to be a runaway hit, but it paved the way for the project 'Red Dog' (code name for Microsoft Azure), the company's cloud business, which later cornered a significant market share away from AWS (Amazon Web Services). 'Bing would prove to be a great training ground for building the hyper-scale, cloud-first services that today permeate Microsoft,' attests then project leader Satya Nadella. 'Building Bing taught us about scale, experimentation-led design, applied ML, and auction-based pricing.'[49] So, as you see, curiosity has very little downside.

Here are three practical tips on honing curiosity in life: 1) take half-chances with uninhibited enthusiasm; 2) make learning and not earning as an outcome; and 3) move on if it doesn't work, and without regret.

Take half-chances

No interesting opportunity will ever be awaiting, fully dressed up, just for you. And then, why you? Why should you be the chosen one? You need to get through the door when it is a crack open, spot the trend when it is weak, bet on a person when others don't, and get to a place with no clear directions. If you are asking too many questions, it means you just want to be convinced why it's not good for you. Anyway, who's there to answer your questions? Who knows any better?

It's the half-chance that Amazon took with allocation of computational power to internal teams that eventually became AWS. Reflecting on the wild success of AWS, Bezos notes, 'No one asked for AWS. No one. Turns out the world was in fact ready and hungry for an offering like AWS but didn't know it. We had a hunch, followed our curiosity, took the necessary financial risks, and began building— reworking, experimenting, and iterating countless times as we proceeded.'[50]

It was his second spell with the semi-old ball amid strong winds when the legendary Imran Khan invented reverse swing. In the historical 1982 match against India in Karachi, the Pakistani pacer created one of the most important exploits with the red ball.[51] And this style became the mainstay of Pakistani cricket, further employed by the likes of Wasim Akram and Waqar Younis. As for India, it was a half chance that selectors offered M.S. Dhoni to lead a rookie team to South Africa for the inaugural T20 World Cup and he came back having made history.[52]

To take half chances in life, you must exhibit unbridled energy and limitless enthusiasm. 'Remain spirited, joyful and curious . . . and the universe will take care of everything else,' writes Robin Sharma.[53]

Let learning take precedence over earning

But so much of curiosity for what? For money? Not always. Your curiosity will serve you only till the time you put learning before earning, means before the end. If you view every incoming opportunity from the cold statistics of value for money rather than the warmth of passion, you will lose even what you think is yours. The real currency of experimentation is learning per unit dollar and time.

The reason most people fear exploration and curiosity is that they can't escape the tyranny of utility: If it doesn't offer (immediate) money, recognition or any other means of gratification, then why bother? Perhaps that's why a research temperament is missing in Indian organisations, for we are often playing to the tunes of the markets. At a personal level, if you understand that where you learn from needn't be the same as where you earn from, you will be more exploratory.

Sam Walton would spend most of his time travelling between his various stores and, when abroad, he wouldn't miss a chance to explore a competitor's store. He had arguably seen more retail stores, of any kind, than anyone else. He would always carry his yellow legal pad and a tape recorder. He would shamelessly imitate anything he thought was interesting and then share those experiments during his legendary Saturday morning meetings.

Warren Buffett spends five to six hours a day poring over five newspapers and over 500 pages of corporate reports. Bill Gates reads fifty books a year and is famous for his *Think Week*. Elon Musk devours as many as two books a day. David Rubenstein aims at six books a week.[54] What are these billionaires looking forward to? What drives them? Learning. I can't offer you better evidence on why learning precedes earning, and how curiosity fuels creativity.

Move on if it doesn't work, without regret

Your curiosity will often take you to dead ends. That's why you must learn to forgive yourself and others.

Here's saintly advice from Elizabeth Gilbert on how to deal with failure in the pursuit of new:[55]

> Whatever you do, try not to dwell too long on your failure. You don't need to conduct autopsies on your disasters. You don't need to know what anything means. Remember: The gods of creativity are not obliged to explain anything to us. Own your disappointment, acknowledge it for what it is, and move on. Chop up that failure and use it for bait to try to catch another project. Someday it might all make sense to you—why you needed to go through this botched-up mess in order to land in a better place. Or maybe it will never make sense. So be it.

If your sense of exploring takes you to a difficult spot, remember that life will give you whatever experience is most helpful for the evolution of your consciousness.[56] Life doesn't always offer you what you ask for, but it certainly gives you what you *need*.

Frankly, you don't lose much from your curiosity. You either revolve or you evolve. Curiosity also means that your identity is fluid. Let's explore this aspect a little better.

Retain a fluid identity

Who are you? That's an important question, indeed. But a more vital question is: Who *all* are you? If you choose to define yourself first and foremost with your professional affiliation (I am VP of Engineering at so and so company), then you are defining yourself rather narrowly. What if you are out of favour? Suddenly, your world starts to break around you because you deliberately gave yourself a very narrow identity. If the world is changing fast, how can you afford to maintain a rigid identity? You need to keep a fluid identity.

Arguably one of the most curious minds of the bygone era, Richard Feynman, maintained a fluid identity all through his life spanning seventy years. From age eleven, he had a home lab where he would construct and repair radios. He would often open mechanical and electrical contraptions and then figure out how to fix them. While studying Physics at Princeton, he would audit classes in Biology, write term papers and even make presentations. Explained Feynman: 'I didn't think I was up to doing actual research in biology, so for my summer visit to the field of biology I thought I would just hang around the biology lab and "wash dishes", while

I watched what they were doing.'[57] That adventure got him to cross roads with James Watson, the co-discoverer of the double helix structure of the DNA molecule and, before long, Feynman was delivering seminars on Biology at Harvard.

Though a theoretical physicist, Feynman taught himself Portuguese and Japanese, played bongo drums, made paintings of nude models, became an expert safecracker while at the Manhattan Project, had first-hand experiences and experiments with hallucination, and other rather abominable enterprises. In fact, when he would play drums at bars and pubs, he insisted on never being introduced as a theoretical physicist, let alone a Nobel prize winner. He followed his curiosity, all the while keeping a provisional allegiance to his primary discipline.

A fluid identity makes you learn faster, as you are exposed to higher variation and lesser predictability. This way, you are pushed towards creativity and away from fragility.

Every time you learn something, your brain gets rewired. While learning, your neurons swell, sway and split. As you are reading this sentence, your neurons are in a continuous motion to make sense of it, and hopefully retain it. Your brain grows through an incessant process of frenetic neural outgrowth and furious pruning, that makes information increasingly compact in your head. Alas, you can't increase the size of your skull to learn more; you must simply compress a great deal into that limited space.

Does variation of your physical environment impact learning? Yes, it does.

Akin to how our bodies have evolved through the brutal forces of variation, selection and retention, so did our minds and ideas therein. Charles Darwin discovered that the brains of wild animals are 15 to 30 per cent larger than those of their tame, domestic counterparts.[58] If you are exposed to a more benign and predictable environment, you will resort to fewer coping mechanisms. To learn better, it's a good idea to expose yourself to different situations, and actively seek stimulus from disparate domains. Specialization, as it turns out, may come at the cost of your creativity, because you are not forming new connections across disparate disciplines. That's how—by exposing yourself deliberately to different situations and realms—you avoid being too narrow a specialist.

It's a good idea to delay specialization in your life. Both Federer and Nadal were football players before they chose tennis over their first liking. The deferred specialization helped them develop better dexterity, physical fitness, versatility and a fall-back option. David Epstein, in his book, *Range*, offers a compelling case for delayed specialization. Epstein characterizes the creative types as people who start broad and embrace diverse experiences and perspectives while they progress. Accomplished artists, sportspeople and scientists maintain a substantial 'sampling period' where they try out different domains, instruments, sports and effectively flirt with ideas before committing. 'Breadth of training predicts breadth of transfer,' notes Epstein. 'Learners become better at applying their knowledge to a situation they've never seen before, which is the essence of creativity.'[59]

On how delayed specialization made him a better chess player, India's first chess grandmaster Viswanathan Anand claims, 'I wasn't browbeaten into picking up chess or playing it. My parents left it to me to divide my time between my studies and chess. Their attitude freed up my mind and put me at ease, and enabled me to fall back on either, as it suited me. Chess for me had no pangs or pressure tied to it.'[60] While he kept studies and his interest in astronomy on the side, Anand managed to become national champion by age ten, and was ranked fifth in the world by the time he finished his bachelor's degree in Commerce.

Paul Kalanithi pursued his BA and then MA in English Literature from Stanford University along with a BS in Human Biology. He followed his calling to join the University of Cambridge to study the History and Philosophy of Science and Medicine. Torn between a PhD in English Literature and Medicine, Kalanithi finally settled for the latter at the Yale School of Medicine, where he graduated cum laude, winning the Dr Louis H. Nahum Prize for his research on Tourette's syndrome. As he writes about the intersection of Literature and Medicine, he revealed, 'Literature provided the best account of the life of the mind, while neuroscience laid down the most elegant rules of the brain.'[61] A cover-to-cover reading of his memoir, *When Breath Becomes Air*, offers how seemingly disparate disciplines merge in sublime ways.

Are you defining yourself too narrowly?

I would rather introduce myself as a reader, writer, teacher, singer, guitarist, motivational speaker, chess player, quote writer and collector, fitness enthusiast, a student of meditation and an independent consultant. Music came late in my life, but I am thankful that it came, as it opened new dimensions. Not just music, but any artistic hobby goes a long way in contributing to our cognitive, social and spiritual growth. As a case in point, the earliest known music instrument dates back to about 60,000 years, whereas we got to organized farming only about 12,000 years ago. A clear indication of our priorities.

Let's spend a moment to understand the impact of music on life in general and creativity in particular. Though the research community is far from a consensus on why music exists among humans, here's a useful definition offered by Ian Cross from the University of Cambridge: 'Musics can be defined as those temporally patterned activities, individual and social, that involve the production and perception of sound and have no evident and immediate efficacy or fixed consensual reference.'[62] So, music lies in the ears of the beholder. What is music to me, could be a noise to others (as many can testify about my guitar skills).

The evolutionary utility of music is unfounded, but there is a solid science on how music helps us today. There is sufficient evidence that music makes you a better listener, it boosts your language skills, enhances your working memory, makes you more adept at handling social situations, sharpens your ability to detect others' emotions and makes you more empathetic. Listening to music and playing musical instruments lifts your mood by enhancing dopamine levels, the pleasure-inducing hormone, cuts down on cortisol, the stress-causing one, and boosts oxytocin that helps you socialize better.[63]

My recommendation: let there be a hobby in your life.

Protect your hobbies from your profession

As a child you had hobbies. As a parent you ferry your child from one hobby class to another. How many of these hobbies do you think your child will make a profession out of? Hardly any. And yet you are willing to spend a fortune 'exposing' your child to life. And how about you? Don't you think you deserve a hobby, too? Rather, you may think, why bother if it doesn't get money into the household? (Why have different yardsticks for you and your child on hobbies?) By not having hobbies, you are missing a major part of your life, or perhaps the heart of your life.

You had hobbies as a child, for you didn't have much to occupy you. You had a lot of free time and you improvised with what you had to keep yourself busy. And then came in your school, and then higher studies, then tuitions, then coaching classes, then college and, before you realized, you were a part of a large assembly line. And now your hobbies have been replaced, sadly, by your profession. And that's not okay.

A hobby offers you three benefits. Firstly, it gives you self-confidence, that there is something which you are good at and with no demand to prove yourself over and over again. You can set your pace, be your audience and your judge. It doesn't have any ultimate objective, except for the very act. Secondly, a hobby offers your different perspectives in life. It lets you connect with people from outside your work sphere, gets you to different places, and to appreciate how rich and diverse the world really is. Lastly, hobbies help you develop new skills, which not only fend off boredom, but also keep you mentally and emotionally agile. At the very core, you make progress on something that you are intrinsically motivated at and want to be better at.

Einstein once said that if he were not a physicist, he would well be a violinist. In fact, latest research on Einstein's 'smuggled' brain hints at the irrefutable link between his proficiency as a violinist and his ability as a mathematician and theoretical physicist.[64] Thomas Edison entertained himself by reading and performing chemistry experiments in his basement lab.[65] Alan Turing would indulge in long-distance running and often ran the forty miles between Bletchley Park and London for meetings.[66] Henry Ford loved crafting and building watches for his loved ones and friends. Gandhi sought respite in gardening and experimenting with medicinal values of plants. Mandela drew inspiration from boxing and long-distance running. And Dhoni likes collecting and driving fast bikes. It keeps them going.

Don't just look at hobbies from a narrow aperture of your work life, but your life after work. Whoever you are or whatever you do, you will retire some day. But your life won't retire you. You will still have to remain relevant, at least to yourself. And that day, your hobbies will come to your rescue. Do you think you will be able to feign a new interest then? Not really. Why not start today? Hobbies can give you a reason to carry on with life.

But never oblige your hobby to pay your bills.

Once you start getting better at what you love doing (call it a hobby), you tend to make something extrinsic out of it. You are eager to exhibit it, put it under public scrutiny and, in the worst case, put a dollar figure to it. And that's where it results in more stress than pleasure. Making a profession out of your hobby is not a bad idea, but better still is to keep a hobby as it is. In fact, many people gave their hobbies a long leash before converting them into something of economic value. People stuck to their calling well before they drew money out of it.

On how he remained committed to his day job while writing books on the side, Nassim Nicholas Taleb admits, 'I for my part spent twenty-three years in a full-time, highly demanding, extremely stressful profession while studying, researching, and writing my first three books at night;

it lowered my tolerance for career-building research.'[67] Taleb was an option trader and an applied mathematician. While trading, he gave us the remarkable treats of *Fooled by Randomness* and *The Black Swan*. Only later did he decide to pursue writing full-time.

For the first seven years of Nike's (then, Blue Ribbon) journey (1962–69), Phil Knight would continue working full-time elsewhere. A Certified Public Accountant (CPA) by qualification and an MBA from Stanford, Knight would first work with the accounting firm Coopers & Lybrand, and later with Price Waterhouse. He would also be a First Lieutenant Knight, clocking in fourteen hours a month soldering in the Reserves, all this while keeping his start-up afloat. Knight confesses that he was putting in six days a week at Price Waterhouse, and then spending early mornings and late nights and all weekends and vacations at Blue Ribbon. Even when Blue Ribbon was raking in a couple of millions in sales, the co-founder didn't want to burden the nascent start-up and instead joined Portland State University as an assistant professor of accounting.[68] Only after a decade or so of starting, did he join his own company full-time.

The novelist, Elizabeth Gilbert, kept on writing alongside her several gig engagements. Her first three books were written this way: stealing time from a day-job. All three were received favourably by the *New York Times*, and one was even nominated for the National Book Award. For most others, that must be it—time to kick the safety net. But Elizabeth just didn't do it. It took the wild success of *Eat Pray Love* for her to quit all other work and be a full-time writer.

As Elizabeth narrates in her book, *Big Magic*, 'I held on to those other sources of income for so long because

I never wanted to burden my writing with the responsibility of paying for my life. I knew better than to ask this of my writing, because over the years, I have watched so many other people murder their creativity by demanding that their art pay the bills.'[69]

It's important to shield your hobbies from your professional demands and let them have a life of their own. A day job can keep your creativity and inspiration flowing. If they converge, good for you, but if they don't, just keep at it. And, finally . . .

No discipline, no creativity

Discipline has got a bad rep. Especially when it comes to creativity. We somehow have been fed with the false premise that the creative types are rule-breakers, or crazy fellows who don't care about others or establishments. It almost gives the impression that creativity is anarchy. But if you care to study further and scratch the surface with a critical mind, then you will discover that creative people are the most disciplined.

The psychiatrist and author of the book, *The Road Less Travelled*, M. Scott Peck, defines discipline as a 'system of techniques of dealing constructively with the pain of problem-solving—instead of avoiding that pain—in such a way that all of life's problems can be solved.'[70] He offers four techniques for bringing discipline in life: delaying gratification, assumption of responsibility, dedication to the truth of reality, and balancing. The following example is a testimony to how discipline can be achieved through these techniques.

Roger Federer attributes his transformation from a raquet-smashing brat to one of the most elegant in the world of sports to the advice and nudge by his fellow Swiss, Martina Hingis. As Federer admits, 'Martina was partially the one who showed me how it was all done . . . It made me also believe with hard work and dedication you get really far, because I didn't believe it that much at that point when I was younger, I thought it was more all talent.'[71] Ergo, even with natural talent, you need discipline to hone it and do something worthwhile with it.

Yet others believe that Federer changed when his Australian coach Peter Carter died in a car accident at age thirty-seven. In an emotional revelation to his friend Andy Roddick, Federer shares, 'Carter for me was a very important figure. He was like a bigger brother for me, almost like a father figure. [His death] shook me, it woke me up and made me realize how fortunate I am to be a tennis player and how much he would want me not to waste anything and I think this is when my career sort of went into overdrive and I want to make Peter proud even though he's not with us anymore today.'[72] Once again, we see that talent, coupled with discipline, triggered by life situations, can transform people.

Many lament that *if only* I had more time and more resources and more guidance, I would have been more creative. The 'if only' rant goes on. But think about it: If they had it all, who needs you? Your value shines amid the deficiency of other critical resources, and that's what resourcefulness is, entrepreneurship is, creativity is. Your ability to get through with whatever little you have and being disciplined in the pursuit of the new. Jeff Bezos maintains that the true hallmark of entrepreneurs and innovators is resourcefulness, and only situations teach you that skill.[73]

The tale of ISRO is that of resourcefulness and discipline. Our resourcefulness is world-famous, for we achieved the Mars Orbiter Mission (MOM) at an expense that beats Hollywood's budget for the movie *Gravity*.[74] The discipline, however, is the behind-the-doors stuff. As for frugality, we had little choice, with no country willing to supply us with technology or the know-how of designing satellites, fabricating rockets, or fuelling those with cryogenics.

In 1962, India sent its first batch of engineers and scientists to NASA to get trained in rocketry. (That very year we had lost a bloody war to China.) One of those engineers, R. Aravamudan, reflects: 'In fact, the entire training offered to us by NASA was what was normally given to an operator or technician. We learned nothing related to design or engineering. No theory was taught, there was very little instruction, and we were mostly left to handle the equipment on our own. In retrospect I realize all our learning was done on our own after we returned!'[75]

The choice was to either be a slave to the mighty or to be a master of our own fate.

We learnt all this the hard way, through a series of failures, often in full public view. Every single expedition of ISRO is telecast live to millions across the world. Where do you see such public display of high-stake experiments? After all, a thousand things can go wrong before, during and after a launch, and even a few months hence, as seen with the failure of India's Chandrayaan-2 landing on the lunar surface. The discipline is in reviewing every single failure, documenting, learning, fail-proofing and then relaunching.

Here's a peek into how discipline gets cultivated at a place where science means no hierarchy. A typical scene from ISRO's Mission Readiness Review (MRR) meeting:[76]

> As one of the senior engineers finishes his presentation, a voice from the last row raises an issue. It is a junior engineer. There is absolute silence as everyone in the room gives him a patient hearing. The engineer who is making the presentation takes notes and gives a detailed response. It really does not matter that the questioner is quite junior in the hierarchy, for in that hall there is absolute technical democracy and no voice is stifled. Everyone knows that many an important issue has come to light at an MRR and at times major failures have been averted because someone raised a pertinent question.

Where else do you see such meetings in the corporate world, let alone government agencies? That's discipline for you.

Unfortunately, we often reduce discipline to punctuality. Punctuality is only one aspect of discipline. It's about being on time. But discipline is a far bigger deal. It's about making the tough choices whenever life puts you at a crossroad. If you promised yourself to get up for jogging early in the morning and the alarm goes off and you tuck back into your blanket; that's lack of discipline. You committed to take your daughter for cycling in the evening and your boss schedules a meeting and you fail to say 'no' to your boss; that's lack of discipline. Nothing to do with punctuality here. It's about taking the high road. Thinking long-term when the short-term is so compelling. And creativity, of all the acts of mankind, calls for discipline the most, for almost always the short-term cost weighs over the long-term benefit. And that's why true acts of creation are so rare. Because discipline itself is so rare.

Creativity is the yin and yang of order and chaos. Without chaos nothing evolves, and without order nothing stays. It's not all chaos, for then you don't know what creativity is. A novel composition is only as good as it fits into the broad rules of the music, but still with a new pattern. Think of a sandbox, where its boundaries give meaning to the sand and the play.

One of the most creative types in the industry, director Christopher Nolan, shares, 'The only useful advice I ever got is to give yourself a script and hang on to it. It's that idea, that screenplay, that concept that's so important and you have to stick to your guns. You have to find something that you can do that maybe other people couldn't do, and even if that seems different or doesn't fit into people's expectations. That's what is going to distinguish it, if you can do it successfully.'[77] Only when he is stubborn on the script and disciplined enough to not take a shortcut that he is able to push his skills and the cinematic experience of his audience.

The yin and yang of creativity also means that for you to be incredibly creative in one aspect of your life, you must deliberately keep the other aspects predictable and almost boring. If you seek excitement in all realms of your life, than you are not only stressing yourself but also being too demanding on your talent and that of those around you.

On the aspect of how predictability liberates creativity, Sam Walton admits:[78]

In many of my core values—things like church and family and civic leadership and even politics—I'm a pretty conservative guy. But for some reason in business, I have always been driven to buck the system, to innovate, to take things beyond where they've been. On the one hand, in the community, I really am an establishment kind of guy; on the other hand, in the marketplace, I have always been a maverick who enjoys shaking things up and creating a little anarchy.

And the greatest contributor to that stability and predictability, I think, is your family. If you have a stable family and peace at home, you can conquer the world. Or else, all your riches mean nothing. You lose the perspective—the context—that makes things meaningful.

Another aspect of disciplined creativity is that it calls for solitude—the 'my time'. 'All creativity comes out of inner spaciousness,' reminds Eckhart Tolle.[79] And this happens when there is a conscious gap in your constant stream of thoughts and behaviours. In solitude you get to talk to yourself, and such inner dialogue, explains the journalist Kate Murphy, 'fosters and supports cognitive complexity, that valuable ability to tolerate a range of views, make associations, and come up with new ideas.'[80]

Your hobby is that 'my time', the solitude that you deserve. If you always surround yourself with people, however wise, you won't have any original thoughts. All your ideas, perspectives, words and deeds will be second-hand. Fear not being alone with your thoughts, to synthesize, to conceptualize, to actualize, for in solitude you are least alone. 'And space and silence are necessary because it is only when the mind is alone, uninfluenced, untrained, not held by infinite varieties of experience, that it can come upon something totally new,' asserted Krishnamurti.[81]

As for discipline, you pretty much have two choices: either you discipline yourself or somebody else does it to you. I guess, the choice is pretty simple.

3

Own Your Career, or Somebody Else Will

*'The problem of distinguishing what we are and what
we are not responsible for in this life is one of the greatest
problems of human existence.'*

—M. Scott Peck[1]

Have you ever spotted yourself sitting in a meeting just to
please those around, especially the higher ups? Worse still,
biting your tongue even when you have a valid point to
make. You eschew the minor risk of making a comment,
lest it might jeopardize your career. Do you join weekly calls
where you are yelled at, motivated by hollow words, when
what you actually need is more time? Do you pick up your
boss's call on a Saturday morning, week after week, for you
must? If yes, congratulations, you are in the majority. It's
such a big majority that it doesn't seem awkward, till it is
pointed out. You do so not for the love for your company
or humanity (at least not always), but owing to the fear of
missing out, or the greed of getting more. And if you think
your behaviour will change once you get promoted, think

again. All such habits will further intensify. After all, you got to this by getting promoted.

When you are willing to sacrifice your private time for an organizational cause, not as an exception but as a routine, you know that you are cheating yourself. But you justify it, stating that you are doing so for your future, of that of your family and the other higher order stuff. But what you don't realize is that while your promotion or other goodies are notional and into the future, what you are willingly sacrificing is real and in the present. You are taking that moment away from your child, your spouse, yourself, or your future self, for something which you rarely control. There must be a better reason for your personal sacrifice than your professional growth.

Here's a thought experiment. Suppose you have a demanding boss, unreasonably so, and you desperately need a raise. What will you be doing? Most likely, you will sacrifice yourself and those around you on the altar of his office. Your weekends are gone, your late evening calls are a norm, your vacations are a distant past, and your health suffers. But one grace. That your boss is happy with you. Or, so you think. In your mind, you reconcile that all of this sacrifice is for the larger good.

Just a week before your appraisal, you get to hear from somebody that your boss has left the organization. Now, how do you feel about it—cheated, frustrated, let down, unlucky? Or do you resign to your fate? Don't you feel like a big fool? Whether you get promoted or not in the new regime is something only time or the new boss will tell, but all that's foregone ain't coming back. This thought experiment might just be a prophecy. Just wait.

In a corporate context, you often operate from a position of 'learned helplessness', a term that psychologists Steven Maier and Martin Seligman define as 'uncontrollability of aversive events'.[2] You feel that you can't change the course of negative events, and that failure is inevitable and unsurmountable (sounds familiar?). Surprisingly, even those in power get trapped into the spiral of learned helplessness as they watch their calendars being booked days in advance. It's hard to believe that the otherwise mentally sharp and morally sound people behave so miserably once they are institutionalized. Why blame others? It happened to me for a long time while I was working during mid-2000s, playing a small role in a large organization. And now, as an independent consultant, when I witness scores of brilliant people fighting pointless battles, I can't comprehend the colossal waste of talent, all for some temporary gains. Certainly not worth it.

There is only one person responsible for your current predicament, your learned helplessness—and it's you. If you think your boss, or worst still, your HR, is accountable for your career and emotional well-being, you are utterly mistaken. Your career is your responsibility. Period. And the sooner you realize this, the better it is for you. Because the next time you check, your HR might well be a machine.

On owning your career, one case study that comes to mind is that of Arundhati Bhattacharya, the first female chairperson of State Bank of India (SBI). Her story is nothing short of inspirational. From a humble beginning as a Probationary Officer at the small Kharagpur branch of the bank, she rose to becoming the first woman chair of the 200-year-old institution, in October 2013. Very skilfully, she balanced the demands of a job that got her transferred every few years and a daughter with disabilities who needed constant medical attention and support. Her leadership saw the bank embrace cloud computing and fintech solutions, rollout the YONO app, launch user-experience labs, internal communication and collaboration platforms, prudent risk management solutions, and engagement with start-ups. She was instrumental in enabling the world's largest financial inclusion programme, Pradhan Mantri Jan-Dhan Yojana (PMJDY), deftly managed the demonetization issue in 2016, and a smooth merger of the seven affiliate banks into one SBI.

Most would lead a comfortable retired life after a leadership role at SBI, but Arundhati was far from it as she reskilled herself to head the India operations of Salesforce. It's an incredible shift from a thirty-six-year career at a state-run bank to the helm at the fast-paced tech world. Not to mention the zeal to remain relevant in the male-dominated financial services space. 'Arundhati is a trailblazer in every sense—she inspires everyone around her, she mentors and empowers the next generation, and leads with courage and integrity, both within Salesforce and across the Indian business landscape,' opines Salesforce CEO Marc Benioff.[3] Some of my friends at Salesforce vouch for her curiosity and sincerity, and that her learning agility is truly remarkable.

So, here's how you go about taking your career by the horns.

Your body is an asset, and not a resource

In the beginning, we had land, labour and capital as the three factors of production. You rent out your land if you have any or, more accurately, if your ancestors had any; then you part with your free will and offer your physical and, later, mental labour, to the more powerful ones; and if you are lucky enough, you invest your capital for a better future. The one who pools all of this is the entrepreneur, who is often considered as the fourth factor of production, and then came along technology which makes the inventor a critical player. Each of these five factors—land, labour, capital, entrepreneurship and technology—have a fair extent of mutual interchangeability between them, as is evident from the surge in the start-up activities in the country. The recently rich are not endowed with land or massive capital but have put their labour into the enterprise of creating and leveraging technology.

But a good 90 per cent of people around you, perhaps including yourself, build their entire careers on labour as a factor to yield returns. They rent their time and talent towards higher order causes and get a share of the spoil. The more the education, the greater the rental, but at any rate, it's the money value of time for most rather than the time value of money. As a result, human resources as a term has stuck with us, legitimized by the corporate machinery and even personal reaffirmations. You assume that you are (just) a resource, in service of a larger cause. The scenes from Charlie Chaplin's classic *Modern Times* won't be a stretch, except that the big machine, which you are a part of, isn't all that apparent.

But let me offer you this thought: *You are not a resource to be consumed but rather an asset to be preserved.* Your body, possibly the asset with highest appreciation, offers you remarkable returns, and has to be taken utmost care of. Think about it; the only possession that you carry all the way to your funeral, quite literally, is your body. It's not your money, titles, accolades, relationships, misgivings or even praises; it's just your body. So why not be a lot more serious about it?

Warren Buffet teases his young listeners with a very meaningful parable:[4]

> Let's say that I offer to buy you the car of your dreams. You
> can pick out any car that you want, and then when you get
> out of class this afternoon, that car will be waiting for you
> at home. There's just one catch: It's the only car you're
> ever going to get . . . in your entire life. Now, knowing
> that, how are you going to treat that car? You're probably
> going to read the owner's manual four times before you
> drive it; you're going to keep it in the garage, protect it
> at all times, change the oil twice as often as necessary. If
> there's the least little bit of rust, you're going to get that
> fixed immediately so it doesn't spread—because you know
> it has to last you as long as you live.

You get one body and one mind for your life, so why not be more nurturing and less abusive towards them? After all, no health=no life, and no life=no career.

This argument becomes very compelling when your health suddenly starts deteriorating. Your entire life changes in one moment.

When diagnosed with an advanced stage cancer, the thirty-six-year-old Paul Kalanithi, a saviour for many such patients, reflected that his relationship with statistics changed the moment he became one. 'I began to realize that coming in such close contact with my own mortality had changed both nothing and everything. Before my cancer was diagnosed,

I knew that someday I would die, but I didn't know when. After the diagnosis, I knew that someday I would die, but I didn't know when. But now I knew it acutely.'[5] That's how unpredictable life is.

One of the big controllable factors that will determine the state of your mind and body in the years to come is your sleep.

Evolutionarily speaking, our natural rhythm is a long sleep at night and a short midday nap (yes). Sleep is not so much for the body as for the brain to organize itself and carry out numerous important functions in a kind of offline processing mode. Many people lead their lives in a way that they carry a massive 'sleep debt' which manifests in more visible problems as they age. 'Sleep loss hurts attention, executive function, working memory, mood, quantitative skills, logical reasoning ability, general math knowledge,' notes John Medina, a developmental molecular biologist.[6]

On sleep, it's pretty straightforward: between not eating anything and not being allowed to sleep, it's the latter that will kill you first.[7] One of the vestiges of the industrial revolution is the eight-hour workday—twenty-four hours divided into three shifts. You work for eight, you sleep for eight, and rest is for your other chores and to keep the show going. But today, both eight hours of work and eight hours of sleep have become exceptions. Travelling to work and working takes way more than eight hours a day, and I don't have to cite research to buttress this point. You experience it, daily.

It's important to prioritize your sleep over almost anything else. Jeff Bezos is very particular about sleeping for eight hours and he claims that it makes him feel better and think better. He opines that it's prudent to make three good decisions a day rather than a hundred low-quality decisions and that sleep deprivation severely impairs decision-making.[8] Even Elon Musk, who is known for his all-nighters and sleeping under his desk to maximize productivity, has learned the hard way to squeeze in at least six hours of daily sleep.[9]

During my engineering days, I would always make it a point to sleep eight to nine solid hours before every exam. Studying all through the year and, more importantly, making copious notes, helped me develop a decent understanding of concepts and practice. I would revise my notes, have a light dinner, take a stroll, and then go straight to bed. Back then, I wasn't aware of the science behind how sleep impacted creativity, but my results were aligned. The result: I would be less stressed before and during the exams.

But when I landed at NITIE Mumbai, things changed dramatically. Hostel life caught on to me. I got involved in so many event teams and office committees that late-night meetings and study groups became a norm, and I could barely manage to sleep for more than six hours on most nights. My studies suffered. But all of this came with a fantastic side effect—I became a good public speaker. I was the first choice for the induction programmes for incoming batches and most other affairs. The same happened years later at IIM Bangalore during my PhD programme where every time I did a night-out to write an assignment or churn out a term paper, I did poorly. So, my experience has been that cutting down on sleep has never helped me.

Even midday power naps for about twenty to thirty minutes can go a long way in helping boost productivity. If your brain at 3 p.m. isn't helping you concentrate, don't kill the urge with a coffee or a smoke; just put your head down on the desk and take a nap. While writing this book, I have been mostly at home. No travels, hardly any workshops, just reading and writing. And twenty minutes of afternoon naps have gone a long way in taking me through the day, for writing is intellectually very demanding. Even for the less demanding ones, don't resort to a coffee.

Here's an interesting finding from the research carried out at NASA: Pilots who slept in the cockpit for twenty-six minutes showed alertness improvements of up to 54 per cent and job-performance improvements by 34 per cent, compared to pilots who didn't nap.[10] Even as some of the most hard-working people in the world, the Japanese put a premium on power naps. They have a word for it—*inemuri*—which roughly means 'sleep while being present'. Afternoon naps at subways, coffee shops, canteens, offices and most public places are legitimate in Japan, and that's perhaps one of the secrets of their superior productivity, problem-solving skills and life expectancy. Google has Nap Pods and Microsoft has Tree Houses at their offices that give a thumbs up to power naps, and they see benefits in well-rested employees.

A well-rested mind can do wonders. Alas, we have little problem finding ways to keep our minds busy, which is literally struggling to get a break from the incessant stream of junk (we call entertainment). So, how to improve the quality of your sleep? Three practices that have served me well: 1) read at least ten pages of something, anything in physical format, before going to bed; 2) always sleep in the dark and invest in a good quality mattress; and 3) keep your phone away from your bed. If need be, buy an alarm clock. That's cheap compared to the assault of your phone.

As a bonus, exercise regularly. Our ancestors walked a lot. By some records, they were on their feet for almost twenty miles a day. And that's how our neocortex was shaped—by being physically active. But if your present lifestyle is predominantly sedentary, you are not only damaging your body but also your mind. One of the greatest predictors of your longevity is whether you have a sedentary lifestyle or not.

Of the several benefits of exercising regularly, research suggests that physical activities can lower the risk of major illnesses like coronary heart disease, stroke, type 2 diabetes and even cancer, and lower your risk of early death by up to 30 per cent.[11] An aerobic exercise improves your problem-solving abilities, fluid intelligence and even memory, and it helps you fend off dementia and depression.[12]

Start with twenty minutes of a jog, every alternate day. Yoga will be beneficial too. But be at it. For as long as you are going back to exercising, you should not mind the breaks.

We next talk about how to propel a body and a mind well taken care of.

The time for passion is now

Till about a few years back, talking of 'following your passion' in an Indian context would have been futile, for you really didn't have much of an outlet for what you liked doing. But that's no longer true. The market has truly opened; people are willing to back you, especially in tier-1 cities, and your mistakes can be overlooked, at least by others. But all this still demands excellence. And excellence, my friend, is in doing the boring stuff well.

Following your passion starts by knowing your passion and as Robin Sharma quips, 'People who study others are wise but those who study themselves are enlightened.'[13] So, let's delve deeper into this seven-letter word.

Here's my definition: Passion is anything that you do without any external motivation. Put differently, passion is something that you don't get tired doing. It doesn't have to be profound or noble. Watching movies, gossiping, cleaning your house, chatting with friends, window shopping—any of that could be a passion. The interesting thing, however, is that 'passion is blind'. While it can drive you, it can also quickly exhaust you.

Passion without reason can certainly waste you. A teacher is passionate and so is a murderer, but for entirely different causes. Said Khalil Gibran, 'Your reason and your passion are the rudder and the sails of your seafaring soul.'[14] While your passion propels you, your reason directs you. Passion comes from heart, reason from mind. We need both, especially a true, internally inspired passion. 'Passion that is not the result of some commitment or attachment, passion that is not lust,' suggested Krishnamurti.[15]

Your passion can be infectious—for your team, organization and even customers. Identifying himself as someone who is excited by ideas and grounded by empathy, Satya Nadella is passionate about putting empathy at the centre of everything he pursues.[16] As he took on the leadership at the struggling Microsoft in February 2014, the company was deeply fragmented, characterized by a 'know-it-all' culture. But over the years, Nadella turned around the once-pioneer into a technological magnate and into a 'learn-it-all' culture.

Nadella deems a company as a vehicle to channelize individual passion for the larger good, and in the case of Microsoft, it's about building products that empower others. So, you see, passion is not just a private affair; it can rally troops, provided you display it viscerally.

Kalanithi was passionate about writing, for he always contemplated between excelling in neurosurgery-neuroscience or becoming a full-time writer. But the diagnosis of cancer at age thirty-six changed his calculus, and what he produced in his last few months is arguably one of the finest pieces on spirituality. His memoir, *When Breath Becomes Air*, left Bill Gates in tears.[17] It's almost of the same gravitas as Viktor Frankl's *Man's Search for Meaning*.

But let's see what passion looks like towards the end of your otherwise very promising career. On Kalanithi's writing regime, Lucy, his estranged wife, remembers:[18]

> Paul wrote relentlessly, fueled by purpose, motivated by a ticking clock. He started with midnight bursts when he was still a neurosurgery chief resident, softly tapping away on his laptop as he lay next to me in bed; later he spent afternoons in his recliner, drafted paragraphs in his oncologist's waiting room, took phone calls from his editor while chemotherapy dripped into his veins, caried his silver laptop everywhere he went. When his fingertips developed painful fissures because of his chemotherapy, we found seamless, silver-lined gloves that allowed use of a trackpad and keyboard. Strategies for retaining the mental focus needed to write, despite the punishing fatigue of progressive cancer, were the focus of his palliative-care appointments. He was determined to keep writing.

Only passion can take you through the most difficult phases of your life. Passion gives you a sense of joy, a drive to pursue something bigger than yourself. And this joy is very much personal. Others may wonder at your enthusiasm as unwarranted, but don't bother; you don't owe anything to most others. While I play my guitar at street corners for it delights me, most passers-by don't bother with a first look. Perhaps that's how I developed a thick skin.

Here's a real testimony of passion. Twelve North American writers have won the Nobel Prize in Literature between 1901 and 2015, and yet none of them had an MFA (Master of Fine Arts). Four of them never even got past high school. Neither Quentin Tarantino nor Christopher Nolan, two of the finest directors of our generation, ever went to a movie school. Maybe that's why.

'I'm a self-taught filmmaker. I never went to film school. I never studied filmmaking,' admits Nolan. 'I started making films when I was seven years old. Making films using my dad's super 8 camera and action figures doing stop-motion films. A little bit of animation and a certain amount of live-action and I just carried on making films as I grew up and, over the years, they got bigger, hopefully better.'[19]

Acknowledge that passion drives the purpose, and not the other way around. If you are driven, then you will find the means, including expertise, if necessary.

Sam Walton, the founder of Walmart, writes in his memoir, *Made in America*, that his primordial passion is to compete. Building one of the world's most prominent business empires out of the small town of Arkansas, Walton suggests, 'Believe in it more than anybody else. I think I overcame every single one of my personal shortcomings by the sheer passion I brought to my work. I don't know if you're born with this kind of passion, or you can learn it. But I do know you need it. If you love your work, you'll be out there every day trying to do it the best you possibly can, and pretty soon everybody around will catch the passion from you—like a fever.'[20]

What propels me? Reading, writing and teaching. And it's virtuous. I am lucky to be able to do it daily, and better still, get paid for it.

Let me highlight three attributes of passion.

Firstly, don't be perturbed if your passion isn't permanent and it keeps changing over time. It's perfectly all right, for life is giving you precisely the discovery process that you must undergo before you do something remarkable with what genuinely propels you. Sachin so much wanted to be a fast bowler before he became a legendary batter. And as the Master Blaster, or as many call him, the God of Cricket, recounts, 'First it [cricket] needs to have a solid foundation in your heart—and gradually from that solid foundation I believe you start building as you grow up, start playing more matches, play a better standard of cricket; then gradually it finds its way to your brain and you start figuring out how to score runs and how to take wickets. But if cricket is not in your heart then results are not that great.'[21] Find your cricket.

Secondly, don't worry about convincing others about your passion. Your passion is a private affair. It may not get you economic or social value, to begin with, but if you are good at it and you keep at it, you will hit a breakthrough. How about being a cricket commentator while cornering a degree in engineering and then an MBA from one of India's most coveted management institutes, IIM Ahmedabad? Yes, you guessed it. We are talking about Harsha Bhogle. Though not a very accomplished cricketer, by age nineteen, Bhogle was already commentating for the All India Radio. His passion was heard through the mic. In 1992, he became the first Indian commentator to be invited by the Australian Broadcasting Corporation. That was quite a feat for a non-cricketer. And over my growing up years, Bhogle's is the fondest voice on the subject. As he writes in his book, *The Winning Way*, 'Skills can be more easily taught, attitude can't . . . and at the very top is passion, an extraordinary drive, where success and joy come together for win after win.'[22]

Lastly, don't settle till your passion converges with your profession. Though that might have once been too much to ask for, but not any longer. During the 1960s and 1970s, one had to be an obedient government servant or a resourceful merchant during the day and then attend to one's passion post work hours: painting, singing, writing, gardening, playing musical instruments, or what have you. But that's not true anymore. You don't have to live a split life, hoping that when you retire you will engage with your passion full-time and till such time, you keep finding love in your work. No more. You must strive to make a profession out of your passion. And you do it by gaining mastery and showcasing your work. If there's no market for you, create one.

An MBBS by qualification, Devdutt Pattanaik followed his interest in reading religious scripts and mythology before obtaining a diploma in Comparative Mythology from Mumbai University. After dabbling with companies like Sanofi Aventis and Ernst & Young, Pattanaik found his calling at the Future Group as its first Chief Belief Officer. By then his passion and profession were almost approaching singularity, and then he shook up the Indian business and political landscape by bringing his unique perspectives from spirituality to the practice of management. He created a niche for himself from nowhere, all by following and investing in his passion.

You get to your passion, often accidentally, but till such time you must keep tinkering. Often people wait for passion to 'occur' to them, while they forget that they aren't the chosen one. It's always humbling to ask the question 'Why me?' before you ask 'Why not me?' You fumble towards your passion instead of unwrapping it.

In your lifetime, you have a chance to discover your true passion for yourself, strive to be the best at it, and then figure out how to offer value to those around you. And don't settle. Till such time, follow these:

Career as a portfolio of enterprise

On 17 March 2017, a massive fire broke out at the Welcome Hotel in Delhi's Dwarka locality. Among the several guests was the Jharkhand one-day cricket team preparing for the upcoming match at the prestigious Vijay Hazare Trophy. As panic struck the guests early in the morning, there was one man who very calmly ushered all of them to safety and in the most clinical manner. The captain this time was Lieutenant Colonel Mahendra Singh Dhoni from the Territorial Army's 106 Infantry Battalion (Para).

Dhoni, the Captain Cool of India, is arguably the most successful leader of the squad in the limited overs format, but he never let his affiliations or success limit his disposition. The desire to join the Indian armed forces predated his aspiration to play for the national squad, and soon after Dhoni lifted the ICC World Cup in 2011, he was awarded the honorary rank of a Lieutenant Colonel by the Indian Army. Still going strong on the national, international and league formats, especially IPL, Dhoni devoted time and attention to attend Army camps, trainings, missions and made it a point to get some stripes on his shoulders. He did a fifteen-day stint as a part of the Victor Force engaged in counter-insurgency operations in the Kashmir Valley.[23] While staying with the troops in the barracks, the former skipper, who is trained as a paratrooper and has done parajumps from aircraft, would discharge his duties of patrolling, guarding and various other post responsibilities.

On how seriously Dhoni took his charge of the Army post, his friend Colonel Vembu Shankar confides, 'Since he is from the parachute regiment, he had to undergo the basic parachute training course in Agra which is very tough. At the end of it, you will earn the right to wear a para wings badge, which is a coveted badge even amongst the Indian Army personnel.' On the man's schedule, Col Shankar discloses, 'He used to get up at around 4 a.m. in the morning and train till about 2 p.m. In the evening . . . (he had to) visit a lot of establishments, meet people to boost their morale.'[24]

Guess what Dhoni wore while receiving the coveted Padma Bhushan on 2 April 2018? The olive green of the Indian Army. If Dhoni can take time to work shoulder to shoulder with the coveted NSG commandos, be a sentry on night duties, can shoot up to ten different assault weapons with proficiency, and make it a point to visit almost all major Army, Navy and Air Force bases across India, do you think your job is keeping you too occupied? Think again.

Let's bring the discussion to the official level.

How do you feel when you don't have a single meeting scheduled for the day? Not even an email or a call all through a workday? Does it make you feel relieved or concerned? Most people that I have spoken to find the very thought unsettling. All sorts of fears cross their minds, for most people aren't comfortable with 'free' time. They would rather do something, anything, to remain busy, than doing nothing. To be comfortable with the void of nothingness, when you are all by yourself, is the key to slowing down.

If you define yourself very narrowly, you risk becoming entirely useless when the tide turns. Even the most astute would face such downturns. Hence, a portfolio of careers keeps you meaningfully occupied and largely relevant.

Who would you identify Atal Bihari Vajpayee as: a politician, a diplomat, a statesman, a poet, a writer, a nationalist, a fighter? I guess, all of these. After taking on the charge, first for thirteen days, and then thirteen months, Vajpayee became the first non-Congress Prime Minister to serve a full five-year term (1999–2004) in his third innings. Under the term of this three-time Prime Minister, India witnessed five nuclear tests conducted at Pokhran in May 1998 which took America's CIA by complete surprise, the historic bus to Lahore in February 1999, the Kargil War in May 1999, Indian Airlines Flight 814 hijacked to Kandahar in December 1999, Musharraf's Agra Summit in July 2001, the attack on the Indian Parliament in December 2001, the Godhra riots of February 2002, and not to mention that in Vajpayee's term we saw A.P.J. Abdul Kalam being elected as the President of India, the 'People's President', in July 2002. Can't think of a more eventful tenure of an Indian Prime Minister!

Born to a school teacher in Gwalior, Vajpayee was inducted into Gandhian socialism as soon as he went to school. He swung into communism during the Fifties, the Swadeshi movement during the 1960s, he swung far-right during the 1970s and 1980s, turned pro-liberalization during the Nineties, and became the poster boy of capitalism towards the end of his political career. His fluid personality can be gauged by the fact that while a full-time worker (*pracharak*) of the Rashtriya Swayamsevak Sangh (RSS), Vajpayee would indulge in consuming whisky and beef; as a lifelong bachelor, he would stay with his lover Rajkumari Kaul and his adopted daughter Namita for over five decades at his official residence; he would conduct a nuclear test in his second term and invite US President Bill Clinton to India in his third; he would beat Musharraf and his men in Kargil and invite him to Agra; he would speak in Hindi at the United Nations General Assembly in October 1977 and yet mesmerize the business fraternity with his fluent English. He was a man of contrasts.

Vajpayee maintained cordial relationships with those in the Opposition, as much as with his detractors within his own party. India's longest serving parliamentarian notoriously opposed Nehru, rooted for Indira on the successful Pokhran-I nuclear tests, saw the rise of Rajiv, fought a bitter battle with Sonia, and witnessed Rahul Gandhi taking on the reins of the Congress. For over seven decades, he maintained his proficiency in poetry, oratory skills, and his love for literature and nature. A multifaceted person, indeed. No doubt he was one of India's most revered politicians and a true Bharat Ratna.

From a man who loved India, to a man who despised the very idea of India.

Winston Churchill, who was known to have suffered from manic depression, never stopped writing and painting and continued this well into his twilight days. In the 'wilderness years' between 1929 and 1939, when Churchill was staring at a premature end to his promising career in the public office, he produced 233 paintings, twelve books, 242 articles, and 475 speeches. And when, in 1940, he was elected as the Prime Minister of UK, he almost single-handedly tilted the balance in favour of the Allies during World War II. As the two-time Prime Minister admitted, 'The Muse of Painting came to my rescue.'[25] In 1953, Churchill was awarded the Nobel prize. In what? Literature! The citation read: 'For his mastery of historical and biographical description as well as for brilliant oratory in defending exalted human values.' That's how a portfolio of careers keeps you going through the tough patches of your life.

As for my career, I have always attempted to retain overlapping strands. Some offer me learning, others give exposure, and yet others help run the family. As early as 2005, I started teaching formally in B-Schools. Then working with Wipro, I had the luxury of at least two days a week to myself, to explore my interests and sharpen my skills. Instead of hitting the malls or nearby destinations, I would visit colleges, and deliver guest lectures. The income was not great, but the exposure was phenomenal. Soon, I was getting good at teaching and was looking forward to the weekends. Alongside, I began taking up workshops on innovation and creativity with organizations, pro bono, to avoid any conflict of interest with my employer. This helped me sharpen my axe and get more clarity on my passion. My life at Wipro was going well, but there was more to me than the narrow ask.

My well-found confidence in teaching and consulting helped me make up my mind to pursue a full-time PhD programme. At the IIM Bangalore campus, I maintained my touch with the outside world, regularly engaging in teaching and consulting assignments; after all, you need a lab to test out your theories. Most of my clients agreed to be my subjects for the PhD thesis. Mid-way through the PhD programme, I got sufficient confidence to consider starting on my own and that's when, in 2016, Inflexion Point Consulting was born. The primary logic was: I can always be a full-time faculty at age fifty-five, but I can't start a company then. Better do it at thirty-five.

Today, I am involved in the thick of consulting, conduct workshops, teach at B-Schools, mentor start-ups and write. I keep the portfolio vital and never sever connect with academia or research. This keeps me grounded and ever learning. Think of your career progression as a series of inflexion points, rather than progressive steps.

The key to honing a portfolio of enterprise is that you start seeding the new while the old is at its peak and delivering. Never wait for too long. As an illustration, I am offering how I went about it. When my employment at Wipro was going strong, I seeded the teaching and researching competence. When researching was at its prime at IIM-B, the entrepreneur in me was taking shape, and today, the teacher and the entrepreneur live side by side, as I am attempting to become an author of relevance.

Figure 6 presents the career overlaps, and how the portfolio looks like today.

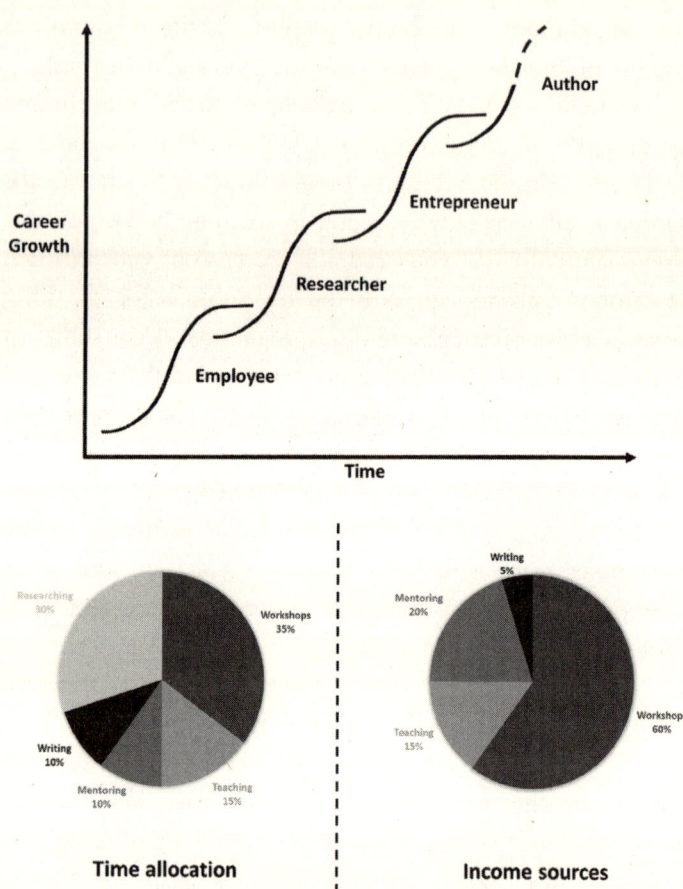

Figure 6: Career as a portfolio of enterprise (my portfolio).

Think of your career as actions to be taken rather than identities to be claimed. It's okay if you haven't made progress on your last assignment or if you didn't manage to secure a career atop your highest qualification. Dump the sunk cost, take a fresh look at your options, and choose the best one. You are not your job; you are always more. Always.

Work hard, but keep tinkering

Most cultures value hard work. In fact, working hard is often deemed as a prime virtue. However, hard work doesn't necessarily involve hard thought. Any paradigm-shifting change, internally or externally, results from hard thoughts. As for this virtue, I will side with Oscar Wilde, who quipped: *Hard work is simply the refuge of people who have nothing to do.*

Angela Duckworth, in her well-researched book, *Grit*, argues that talent is secondary when it comes to achievement; it's the perseverance that counts. She offers the following two equations:

$$Talent \times Effort = Skill$$
$$Skill \times Effort = Achievement$$

In essence, effort has a power effect on achievement, given some talent. Effort, or what she calls grit, has two components to it: passion and perseverance.[26] You know what you want and are willing to go for it, against all odds.

However, this view hides something profound: experimentation. You can keep at something indefinitely, but without bringing the necessary variation you will get pretty much the same results. Dick Fosbury would have killed himself trying the conventional and perhaps the right way to high jump before he experimented with the back-first approach in the 1968 Summer Olympics and changed the game forever. When you look at it, the Fosbury flop seems to be the most natural and ergonomic way of high jumping, but not till our man took the chance. That's the importance of experimentation.

Accordingly, if I may propose:

Grit x Tinkering = Achievement

Our popular media and urban legends conveniently hide risky experiments in the face of hard work, and hard work in the face of sheer talent. Perhaps that's why a lot more people like Federer for his natural effortlessness than Nadal for his palpable grit. We forget how much tinkering Nadal does across the playing surfaces to remain consequential in such high-stake settings. You must learn to experiment, even pivot entirely, if your grit is not taking you too far. Grit may get you killed, as exemplified by the escalation of commitment too often seen in entrepreneurial milieus. 'Sometimes the best kind of grit is gritting our teeth and turning around,' notes Adam Grant.[27] No shame in that.

From a career standpoint, experimentation, or tinkering, is extremely vital. Tinkering not only tells you a lot about yourself but also about the world around you. 'The knowledge we get by tinkering, via trial and error, experience, and the workings of time, in other words, *contact with the earth*, is vastly superior to that obtained through reasoning,' suggests Taleb.[28] He maintains that somebody who tinkers incessantly, keeping what's useful and discarding what's useless, innovates faster than the one who follows a well laid out plan. Innovation is inherently an ambiguous process.

Instead of somebody, including yours truly, telling you what you ought to do, you keep experimenting with your career till you settle for something which has an intrinsic value to you. It will take time, but you will gain confidence in the bargain.

'If you want to go deeply into any subject, you need a lot of time, and in particular you need the privilege of wasting time,' reflects the historian Yuval Noah Harari. 'You need to experiment with unproductive paths, to explore dead ends, to make space for doubts and boredom, and to allow little seeds of insight to slowly grow and blossom. If you cannot afford to waste time—you will never find the truth.'[29] And perhaps that's why most people will be willing to live with answers that cannot be questioned than the questions that cannot be answered. Unfortunately, wasting time is considered a bane in this world obsessed with productivity.

The success of Nike can well be attributed to the relentless tinkering by its co-founder, Bill Bowerman. The famous track and field coach was so passionate about improving the performance of his athletes that he never gave up experimenting with his shoes and the way they fit. 'He'd spend days tearing them apart, stitching them back up, then hand them back with some minor modification, which made us either run like deer or bleed,' recollects Phil Knight, Nike's other founder and Bowerman's protégée. 'Regardless of the results, he never stopped. He was determined to find new ways of bolstering the insteps, cushioning the midsole, building out more room for the forefoot. He always had some new design, some new scheme to make our shoes sleeker, softer, lighter.'[30]

One of these famous designs was the 'Waffle Trainer' (US patent # 3,793,750), designing which Bowerman would destroy several Belgian waffle irons back home, inhale toxic fumes, get injured, but never give up. When the shoe finally became viable in 1974, that one trick helped pull the company ahead of the German Adidas and Puma, and never to look back. Even today, Nike continues to work with top athletes to improve their performance. Rafael Nadal acknowledges how Nike worked around his sour left foot to provide the right cushioning, allowing him to take the stage.[31]

To be a tinkerer, you must hone a thick skin, for if you are too bothered about what others feel or say about you, you will lead a life busy pleasing strangers. Cultures that pride themselves on being 'right first time', being right every time, can't risk innovation and creativity. Apart from being thick-skinned, you must be willing to be wrong. 'It takes confident humility to admit that we're a work in progress,' notes Adam Grant. 'It shows that we care more about improving ourselves than proving ourselves.'[32]

The question is: Do you offer yourself the luxury of failing? Moreover, are you willing to forgive yourself? A lot depends on your financial position. Here's how.

Financial freedom keeps you intellectually honest

Often people ask me: 'Is entrepreneurship for everybody?' My answer is: 'No.' Not everyone can become an entrepreneur. But, yes, anyone can become 'enterprising'. And it pays to be enterprising—going well beyond your call of duty or your job description.

I have had three distinctive phases of my career: as an employee at Wipro, as a researcher at IIM Bangalore, and now as an independent consultant and entrepreneur. Which phase did I enjoy the most? Well, all three. The stint as an employee gave me the clarity that I must invest in myself to be a better teacher and researcher, and that paved the way for the IIM-B PhD. The PhD programme gave me the intellectual heft and the legitimacy to take the plunge into the world of entrepreneurship. But what remained consistent all through is my enterprising nature. My central propeller has been the unyielding need to remain financially independent and for as long as possible, for I believe that financial independence keeps you intellectually honest.

So, in a way, entrepreneurship is not a job title, but a way of life. Further, you don't have to be rich or senior to be enterprising. If anything, these may pose as hindrances. Let's talk about how to become enterprising, in whatever role you play: employee, manager, administrator, student, teacher, politician, homemaker, or entrepreneur.

Don't seek resources, be resourceful

You will largely come across two types of people: the ones who *ask* why not, and others who *justify* why not. If you wish to accomplish something, you don't need too many reasons or even resources, and if you don't, no excuse or resource is sufficient. Looking at the country of Israel, or post-war Japan, or Singapore of the last few decades, it's adequately clear that resource scarcity isn't as much a handicap as an opportunity to be audacious and display chutzpah.

It's not what you have, but what you do with whatever you have, that counts. One of the attributes of the Marwari business community is resourcefulness. The scarcity of material resources is more than compensated by the investments in social capital and frugality as a way of life. Ditto for the Jewish community, which gave education and improvisation the highest weightage, when the chips were down. Engineers and scientists at ISRO, doctors and paramedics at hospitals like Aravind Eye Care and Narayana Hrudayalaya, air and ground staff at IndiGo, our soldiers at punishing heights of the Siachen glacier and those patrolling at LAC and LoC practice resourcefulness as a second nature. So should you.

Be a good salesperson

I reckon that the most non-negotiable skill of being an entrepreneur is selling. As an entrepreneur, you are always in the sales mode: selling a dream to investors, a career to employees, a concept to customers, and glory to yourself. And yet scores of aspirants deem selling as cheap, or below their taste. If you argue that putting your idea to its rightful audience isn't your job, think again.

I haven't come across any successful entrepreneur who shies away from selling. Nor a leader who is not constantly selling a dream up and down the chain of command. Selling is the linchpin between not having and garnering those critical resources. It demonstrates ownership—of your vision, your action and its consequences. In fact, one of the central tenets at Amazon is: Focus on hiring and retaining versatile and talented employees who can think like owners.[33] So, sell with pride, especially if you are the creator.

Seek forgiveness rather than permission

There are just about two attitudes towards your work: right first time, or wrong first time. You have been taught, or rather hammered, to be right the first time and every time. But implicit in this expectation is that you *know* what is right and how to go about it. If you are genuinely trying to do something new, you certainly do not know what to expect, let alone how to go about it. So, you will naturally fail the first time, likely the second time, and only by your fourth or fifth attempt will you have some semblance of being right. And, if you are right the first time while attempting even the slightest of novelty, you are deluding yourself. It means that either you have truly lowballed yourself or that you have manipulated the very definition of success.

Most people cover their risk by seeking permissions or blessings from those in power. This urge for seeking permission even for the most innocuous causes is okay as long as the ask is of continuous improvement or scoring productivity gains. But as soon as the bar is raised, the very same 'obedience' starts to recoil. Douglas MacArthur reminded us that you are remembered for the rules you break. And most Indians at work aren't exactly the role models. Cutting corners is not the same as breaking rules for some higher cause.

The ethos of the enterprising type is: *Better to seek forgiveness than to ask for permission.* Because, frankly, whom are you seeking permission from? The very people who are in positions of authority draw their powers from the status quo and because creativity invariably challenges the status quo, why will they entertain your radical ideas? They will detest it, to the best of their clout. Further, what's the proof that your idea will work? You must, at the least, offer a proof of concept, and to get that far, you should be okay with failing a couple of times, and that's truly the uncharted territory for the most obedient types. So, let 'sorry' come more easily than 'please'.

Pursue and protect your freedom

Resourcefulness is like a leverage; you need to have a solid anchor to be able to pull the lever. It's like you can raise a huge debt if you own the equity (the Marwari community is excellent at it). However, most entrepreneurs don't treat their equity with respect. They are willing to dilute it at a hint of bargain. There is little doubt, a lot of founders are eased out of their own creations as they fail to secure sufficient equity, and then the vagaries of the market take over.

Whether as an entrepreneur or not, you must make your money work towards achieving freedom (not just financial freedom). The freedom to say 'no'. And maintain it. 'If wealth is giving you fewer options instead of more (and more varied) options, you're doing it wrong,' warns Taleb.[34] And you can say 'no' only when you have maintained a portfolio of careers, when you are not dependent on any single source of income or, worse still, an individual.

In short, don't chase resources; instead, try making the most of what you already have, and new directions will open up for you. Leaving you with the ingredient that can't be taught but can only be learnt and displayed: courage.

Don't live on borrowed courage

You must have seen security guards at banks or ATMs carrying double-barrel rifles. It's not an ideal arm for a short-range combat, and yet it does the trick. The guard isn't shooting at somebody in proximity in the bank nor at a bunch of guys running on the streets with the loot. The gun, in fact, serves a more important function: It's a deterrent. The guard is not meant to use the gun, but an unmistakable display does the trick. That's your infallible signal. A pistol or a revolver can pretty much do the necessary damage to the perpetrators, but it doesn't send a reliable signal. The double-barrel gun does.

Where is your double-barrel gun? What is your non-cheap signal? A signal with a very high barrier to secure, but offering an unfailing legitimacy, which is not easy to imitate or bypass. In fact, it's not just a signal, but one which you can indeed act on. It needs courage. I can't teach you courage, I can only demonstrate it. For, courage is the only virtue you cannot fake. It's binary; either you have it, or you don't.

Let's not confuse courage with fearlessness. Being courageous is about bravery in the face of uncertainty, respecting your boundaries and being adaptive to the terrain. As the author Elizabeth Gilbert clarifies, 'Creativity is a path for the brave, yes, but it is not a path for the *fearless* . . . Bravery means doing something scary. Fearlessness means not even understanding what the word *scary* means.'[35] Since every creative endeavour involves risk-taking and it triggers fear, often when people try to kill their fear, they end up inadvertently murdering their creativity in the process.

So, if you are afraid, it's natural. You need courage to keep going.

The question is: Where does courage come from? Who's the mother of courage?

Let me take you through a real-life incident. A couple of years ago, a learning and development professional from a Fortune 500 company reached out to me to help conduct a design thinking workshop for her leadership team. I quoted 'x' amount for the session, upon which she straightaway offered 'x/2'. At first, I couldn't comprehend it. I asked her if they have the budget and if this training programme was a priority for them. To both, she said a 'yes'. Still, she insisted on x/2, stating that it's their business practice: 'You start at x, I start with x/2 and then we negotiate our way to 3/4x.' That's apparently their business logic. After some five minutes of back and forth, I told her, 'I am afraid it will be x, miss. Take it or leave it.' Now, here's the moment of truth; did she take it, or did she leave it?

When I quiz my workshop participants with this question, a good 90 per cent side with 'she took it'. But the reality is that she never took it. I never heard back from them. Should I be okay with it? Certainly, or else I shouldn't have proposed 'take it or leave it!' I should have thought through the consequences in advance.

Going back to the question: Who's the mother of courage? It's 'clarity'.

The clarity of what happens next. Your ability to think through the situation. To be totally honest with yourself. As Krishnamurti insisted, 'I must expose myself to myself—not necessarily expose myself to you because you may not be interested—but I must be in a state of mind that demands to see this thing right to the end and at no point stops and says I will go no further.'[36]

Most of us fear going all the way down the alley of self-discovery. But when you understand the worst that could transpire, you get courage. Till such time, you are living on borrowed *display* of courage. You need to understand your emotions, out and out. 'If you hold back on the emotions—if you don't allow yourself to go all the way through them—you can never get to being detached, you're too busy being afraid,' writes Mitch Albom in his spiritual treatise *Tuesdays with Morrie*.[37]

Once again: Who's the mother of clarity? Where do you get the ability to go further and deep?

If you read the dialogue I had with the lady at the Fortune 500 company, you should ask: Where did I get the clarity that if this client didn't get back, then somebody else would? It came from 'content'. The content that I have garnered through the years of the PhD programme, thereafter with numerous client situations and through the formal and informal networks I have formed, apart from reading wide and deep. Without content there is no clarity, and without clarity there is no courage, as shown in Figure 7. But don't confuse content with knowledge. Think of content as contextual knowledge. Content is the hard-earned differential. As the Zen saying goes, 'Don't seek the truth. Just cease to cherish opinions.' You need to keep that differential positive and relevant at all times.

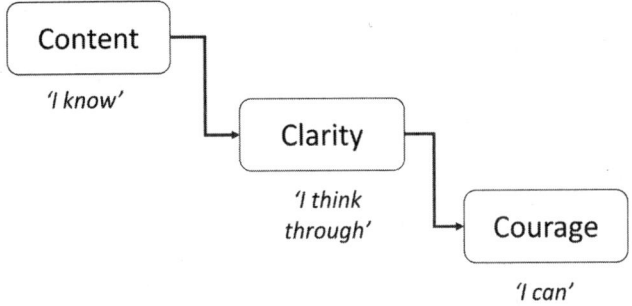

Figure 7: Courage comes from clarity and clarity from content.

So, where do you get the much sought after courage from? You must start with building content. Content, which is substantial, proprietary and relevant. And then you must fear nobody. Here is what courage looks like. Writes Bruce Lee, 'Let things be what they are, move like water, rest like a mirror, respond like an echo, pass quickly like the non-existent, and be quiet as purity.'[38]

Let's look at another thorny issue. What matters more: your content or contacts? For a long time, it was believed, and rightly so, that *who* you know is more important than *what* you know. As the saying goes: 'A good lawyer knows the law but a great lawyer knows the judge.' I wonder if that's true anymore. With the cost of search and transaction coming down drastically over the past few years, if you have solid content, then you can overcome network deficiencies. In other words, if you know your stuff well, people will sniff you out; and if you don't, then they will avoid you.

Take for instance LinkedIn, the professional world's go-to network. If you are a master at something that others value and you present yourself well through high quality content creation, then others will discover you. You are just a click away. And if your content is not of high quality, your network will merely amplify that fact. Where do I get most of my business from? Content, followed by contacts. If I expect my alumni network to refer me or root for me, they must be assured that I have stuff to offer. The mere fact that we studied together a couple of decades ago doesn't cut ice. They will be more hesitant than a stranger if I am not up to the mark, for they will have much more to lose by backing me.

To understand the link between content, clarity and courage, let's look at some real-life heroes.

How do you deal with a double engine chopper, with sixteen people onboard, falling freely through the clouds? A double engine failure is deemed the rarest of rare and that's precisely what pilots at the Indian Air Force are trained to handle. In command was Squadron Leader Vikas Puri and the chopper was the Russian made Mi-17, the versatile workhorse which has proved its worth across numerous wartime and peacetime operations in India, including peacekeeping missions in Africa.

On 12 March 2016, the Mi-17 was carrying sixteen personnel, including the head of the Eastern Air Command Air Marshal Chandrashekharan Hari Kumar, and his wife, on a trip from Shillong, Meghalaya, to two new airfields in Arunachal Pradesh, via Tezpur, Assam. Twenty-five minutes into the flight and at an altitude of 4,500 feet, the onboard emergency system declared 'service tank pump failure'. Sqn Ldr Puri noticed that the chopper was banked on one side and over the next thirty seconds, the generator went cold, both the engines were down, and the helicopter was plummeting on to the paddy fields below at the rate of twelve metres per second.

As the calm and ever alert Sqn Ldr Puri was planning for a safe (crash) landing of a dead chopper, he decided to restart the engine, which he believed died owing to fuel starvation and not a technical failure. He ordered the flight engineer to switch on the fuel bypass valve, and to power the engines using an auxiliary power unit (which would take another thirty seconds to power up). All they had were ninety seconds before they hit the ground. At barely 600 feet and twenty seconds from impact, the captain ordered one engine to be cranked and collective levers to be raised, and the Mi-17 was pulled back from the jaws of certain crash. Moments later, as the helicopter recovered from its auto-rotating flight, the second engine too came alive. All this happened in 120 seconds.[39]

At the eighty-fifth Air Force Day on 8 October 2017, Wing Commander Vikas Puri was bestowed with the Vayu Sena Medal (Gallantry). The citation read:[40]

> In this fearless and courageous effort, he not only saved sixteen invaluable lives but also a precious war-waging asset. He showed exemplary valour, bravery, maturity, exceptional professionalism and situational awareness in tackling one of the gravest emergencies in a Mi-17 helicopter.

Years of training gave him the *content*, keeping himself calm in an adverse situation offered the *clarity*, and then came the *courage* to pull the unthinkable. Without content and clarity, courage stands no chance. It's important to keep your axe sharp at all times, and *your* time will come.

4

Focus on High-Leverage Activities

'Greatness is not a function of circumstance. Greatness, it turns out, is largely a matter of conscious choice.'

—Jim Collins[1]

What's common across the following texts?

Dialogue Concerning the Two Chief World Systems (Galileo Galilei, 1632)

Philosophiæ Naturalis Principia Mathematica (Isaac Newton, 1687)

On the Origin of Species (Charles Darwin, 1859)

Das Kapital (Karl Marx, 1867)

On the Electrodynamics of Moving Bodies (Albert Einstein, 1905)

Science: The Endless Frontier (Vannevar Bush, 1945)

The Structure of Scientific Revolutions (Thomas Kuhn, 1962)

All these books, or papers, pushed our thinking forward, not incrementally, but radically. My favourite is the one from Thomas Kuhn, where he introduces us to the beautiful idiom, *paradigm shift*. These were indeed paradigm shifts. These were high leverage creations, ones that outlived the authors comprehensively.

What is a high leverage activity? It's an act that leads to the creation of an enduring asset, which gains value with time. The act has the following five characteristics: 1) It poses little or no sense of urgency; 2) It has a compounding effect over time; 3) The long-term rewards outlive the short-term penalties or hardships; 4) It offers you a shot at immortality; and finally, 5) It doesn't happen automatically or accidentally. In short, a high leverage activity has a high intellectual property content, which compounds over time.

Now, look at your last week at office, or the last month, or even the bygone quarter. Which activity did you pursue that's going to give you mileage over the long run? Certainly, your hard fought, or hard survived, meetings won't make the cut. Directing, motivating or monitoring people? Not really. Client presentations, or even signing contracts, won't qualify either, for soon enough you are staring at revised targets. Perhaps if you developed or shipped a product, then yes. Or, if you created some solid content that's beyond the flavour-of-the-month, then yes. If you can't distinguish being busy with being *meaningfully* busy, you are doomed to be on the proverbial treadmill of insignificance.

Leverage comes from essentially three attributes: labour, capital and intellectual property. Labour is when you have scores of people working for you, or under you, and you direct them towards a larger cause. This requires constant efforts and vigil, for morale hazard must be kept at bay and the targets are best kept as mirage. Next is capital. As an intelligent investor, with a good starting base and above average decision-making skills, you can do wonders with your capital. The influencers of the bygone era, the Birlas, Tatas, Rockefellers are all masters of leveraging capital and labour. But the new riches are intellectual property.

Intellectual property can take the shape of concepts, artefacts, publications, literature, books, research papers, patents, products, brands or the ideas that become standards. If done well, intellectual property can leave the biggest mark for the longest time. And in this era of pervasive technology and democratization of labour and access to capital, applied intelligence offers the greatest leverage. Investor Naval Ravikant goes to the extent of recommending you to *productize yourself*.[2] The 'productize' part is the leverage with specific knowledge, whereas 'yourself' has accountability where you put your personal skin in the game.

As for me, there are only two high leverage activities that I have done in the last twenty years. Only two. One is the PhD programme from IIM Bangalore, and second is writing the book, *Design Your Thinking*. The returns are remarkable. Did I have to steal time and other resources to carry out these activities? Yes. The PhD programme required me to resign from Wipro and the book meant that I must say 'no' to dozens of workshops and assignments. But the returns more than compensated for those sacrifices, for now I get to operate on a higher plane. It all starts with valuing yourself.

Put a premium on yourself

Why does your boss call you at 10 a.m. on a Sunday morning? The answer is simple: because you pick up the call. If you don't, he won't. The way you treat your time sends a signal to how others should treat your time. If you don't put a premium on your time, nobody else will. So goes the saying, you deserve what you tolerate. If people abuse you repeatedly, it's your mistake, not theirs. You are giving them an excuse to.

Let's revisit the 'Zone of Concern' and the 'Zone of Influence' to understand this further. Your zone of concern comprises all that bothers you. Often, you invite such stuff into your life. It can range from what to have today for lunch, all the way to the fallout of global warming. The more twenty-four-hours news channels you watch and the more Facebook you browse, more expansive becomes your zone of concern. And within this vast panorama is your zone of influence, things that you can actively shape or change for good. There are always way fewer things that you can control or alter than you think. Consequently, your zone of influence is a very tiny subset of your zone of concern.

An expansive zone of concern can make you miserable rather quickly, and since you have a finite capacity and attention, this botheration will mostly come at the cost of your zone of influence. Hence, the recommendation is to consciously shrink your concerns and expand influence, as shown in Figure 8. Worry about fewer and fewer things to the extent that you bother only about what you can shape. Ideally, your two zones should completely overlap—you care only for what you can influence. As Dhoni would say: 1) control the controllables, and 2) no man can have everything in life, there's always that one thing you will never be able to have.[3] So, make peace with it.

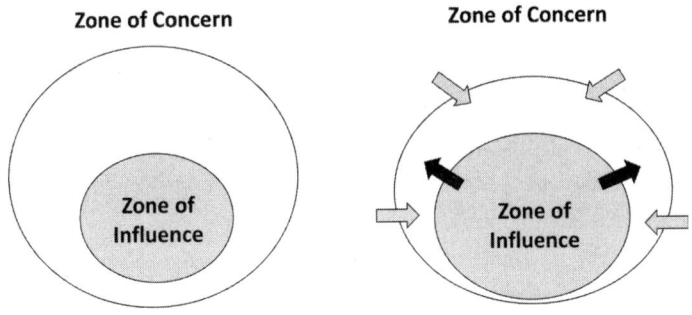

Shrink Your 'Zone of Concern' and Expand Your 'Zone of Influence'

Figure 8: The Zone of Concern and the Zone of Influence in life.

In fact, when you put a premium on yourself, you are concerned only with high leverage activities, and you don't sweat over the small stuff. You don't live in the thick of thin things. You don't major on minor topics. You pick worthy causes, because only then do you withstand resistance or even failure. I distinctly remember my PhD guide warning me that nobody gets out of this programme in less than five years; you can either choose a difficult problem or an easy one. The choice was rather clear. Let's look at doing something substantive, for you don't do a PhD (or most other high-commitment stuff in life) twice.

It also keeps you on a morally high ground, for now you are not seeking ways to keep yourself busy or feel important. As Warren Buffet suggests: Never do anything that you won't like your mother to read in the newspaper. I guess that says it all.

Warren Buffet likes to stick to his 'Circle of Competence'.[4] He would readily say 'no' to an awful lot of opportunities before he would say 'yes' and commit himself. It's the economic logic of the business that must make sense to the billionaire investor before he writes the check. You can always go about exploring the more esoteric areas to invest in, but you are increasing your risk exponentially by doing so. Since most returns are accrued through compounding, it's best to be very selective in your decisions and then stick to the knitting.

As the leadership coach Marshall Goldsmith observes, 'Successful people avoid high-risk, low-reward situations and do everything possible in their power to increase the odds in their favor.'[5] The same story repeats in domain after domain. If you want to stand out, you must be very careful about how to spend your attention, time and efforts. It pays to conserve and converge these precious resources.

On the power of selective response, Viktor Frankl reflects, 'Everything can be taken from a man but one thing: the last of the human freedoms to choose one's attitude in any given set of circumstances, to choose one's own way.' In his book, *Man's Search for Meaning*, Frankl documents how the death rates at the concentration camps soared between the Christmas of 1944 and the New Year. It was not owing to excessive cold or malnutrition or the degradation of living conditions at the camps, but because people lost hope. They hoped to be united with their families at Christmas and when it didn't happen, they lost the desire to live. 'The prisoner who had lost faith in the future—his future—was doomed. With his loss of belief in the future, he also lost his spiritual hold; he let himself decline and became subject to mental and physical decay,' concludes Frankl.[6] You need to be in total control of your zone of influence, regardless of what happens around you.

Ace sportspeople have this ability to cut down their concerns so much that they are razor focused on what really matters.

Sachin could become such a master of the game because he almost never engaged in a verbal duet with the bowler or anybody on the field. He was so effective against West Indians, and later Australians, because they couldn't get him to engage beyond his zone of influence. They couldn't get him to change his plans, and that's what legends are made of—an unnerving concentration in the face of the most challenging adversaries.

When do your zone of concern and zone of influence overlap completely? It's when you are struggling to survive. In modern times, there is one person who has made a life and career out of putting himself in harm's way, instructing us on how to survive in the harshest of the situations, man-made or natural. Yes, I am talking about Bear Grylls, of the *Man vs Wild* fame. As Grylls recollects several of his near-death experiences and reflects on the true grit of people who saw it all and walked through hell, he spiritually offers:[7]

We humans like to surround ourselves with material possessions and convince ourselves that they're necessary to our happy existence. But happiness can sometimes be masked in adversity, and it sometimes isn't until we

lose every comfort we have ever known that we truly appreciate the simple truth: that the best things in life are never bought. Pride, joy, calm, simplicity of existence, and our relationships with those around us, are the greatest wealth we ever own.

And if the pandemic didn't teach you this, you perhaps missed the whole point!

How does the premium work in the corporate context? For that, let's revisit the time-honoured Urgency- Importance Matrix, or the Eisenhower Matrix, albeit with a slight twist, as presented in Figure 9.

	Urgency	
	High	**Low**
High (Importance)	**Disciplined Execution** (1. Managers)	**High Leverage Activities** (2. Leaders)
Low (Importance)	**Confident Delegation** (3. Employees)	**Kill Your Habits** (4. Technology)

Figure 9: Urgency-Importance matrix (revisited).

A quick overview of the matrix: On the y-axis you have the relative importance of a task—high or low, while the x-axis has its urgency—high or low. It gives you four quadrants: 1. Disciplined Execution, 2. High Leverage Activities, 3. Confident Delegation, and 4. Kill Your Habits.

Let's get to the heart of achieving high leverage.

The most fundamental and yet the most misunderstood aspect of the matrix is 'important to whom?'. To be very clear, it's important to 'you', personally. Not to the customer, or your boss, or your firm, or your family, or any other. An equally frequent question is: What should I bother about, the important stuff or the urgent stuff? Well, you must be very clear about what's important to you, because you can't control urgency. But if you don't know and control what's important to you, you rebound from one urgent task to another (sounds familiar?).

Be clear about your pecking order before urgency sets in, for once things start looking urgent you lose your bearing on priorities. As often is the case when you are shouted upon by somebody in authority. Bear in mind that you determine importance, while the situation determines urgency. Don't get played in the hands of the situation. So, I offer:

Conjecture # 1: Control the important, manage the urgent.

Now let's jump right into the matrix. If you deem a task as important for you (and not necessarily for your employer or your family members), you need to prioritize it explicitly. Make it clear to yourself and to others. And when the time comes, learn to execute deftly. If you recognize something as important and the matter has assumed urgent proportions, you need to bite the bullet. Or else you risk losing your self-confidence and credibility.

It's critical to not get drawn into a false sense of importance or urgency. Often everything loud and rushed seems important, but it seldom is. If you look at the last two months of your WhatsApp messages, what percentage of those will you consider important? I bet that it won't be more than 5 per cent. However, when the message arrived, with what urgency did you treat it? I guess, it was above 80 per cent. So, you see, your mind gets tricked into thinking that if it's urgent, it must be important. Discipline is in delinking the two. Let's call this the *Managers Quadrant*. Most managers are good at getting work done, not necessarily knowing the 'why' of it. Sufficient to say:

Conjecture # 2: If it's important, don't drag your feet on it.

Disciplined execution can take you only so far. The trick is to invest time and effort in working towards matters which haven't yet assumed urgent proportions but are nevertheless very important. They are mostly to do with self-development or creating an enduring asset. Thinking long-term and planning for those is indeed a high leverage activity and most people aren't good at it, by themselves. Reading a book, jogging daily, attending a meditation programme, pursuing higher education, investing time with your child on her hobbies, are all high leverage activities. Whether you do these or you don't, your life doesn't change immediately, but it surely does over the long run.

Let's call the high leverage activities the *Leaders Quadrant*. Most leaders are good at thinking long-term, and planning and investing for the long run. So, I propose:

Conjecture # 3: Plant high leverage activities.

We revisit this matrix again while discussing the attributes of delegation.

To put a premium on yourself is to cut down all your concerns, pin your focus on what you can influence and ensure that you make it count. You look at what's really important in the long run, prioritize it and work towards it, while honouring your present commitments. This puts you in a Zen-like state, or what the Hungarian-American psychologist, Mihaly Csikszentmihalyi, famously called 'The Flow'.

High leverage requires flow

Every activity has two dimensions to it: the challenge it offers and your commensurate skills to be able to carry it out. From a career perspective, you can view your day as a series of tasks, each posing a certain demand, cognitively or viscerally, and then the proficiency with which you address it. The broader your zone of concern, the more you feel confronted; not just by the immediate task but also the background and other variables which you care to consider. Think of how traffic on the way to your office can hamper your performance, or an avoidable argument with somebody unrelated can unsettle you. All because you are too concerned about too many things. On the other hand, your skills emerge from your zone of influence, things which you know you can affect. It's worth noticing that both the zones are deliberate.

To sum up, your Zone of Concern offers you challenges, whereas your Zone of Influence provides you skills.

Figure 10 presents an augmented version of the flow channel proposed by Csikszentmihalyi in his landmark work, *Flow*. The y-axis represents the challenge associated with a task, while the x-axis indicates the skills available to address the task. If a task doesn't offer sufficient challenge to absorb your attention and skills, you quickly feel bored (think of an average office meeting); whereas an activity which poses a greater challenge and exposes your lack of skills can certainly make you anxious (much like your first week at work). However, if a certain challenge can absorb all your faculties and you are left with nothing else to think of, then you are in the optimal state, called the Flow Channel.

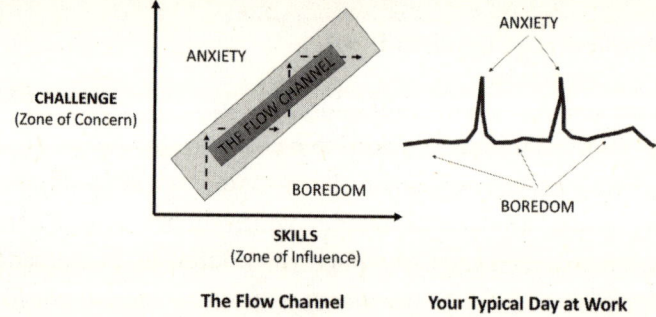

The Flow Channel   Your Typical Day at Work

Figure 10: The Flow Channel (adopted from Mihaly Csikszentmihalyi) and your average day at office.

Csikszentmihalyi defines *flow* as 'the state in which people are so involved in an activity that nothing else seems to matter; the experience itself is so enjoyable that people will do it even at great cost, for the sheer sake of doing it.'[8] Such 'optimal experiences' have the following attributes: 1) you have a chance of completing the task, 2) as you are able to concentrate, 3) on a clear goal, 4) which offers immediate feedback, 5) with an effortless involvement, 6) while you retain a sense of control over the actions, 7) where the concern of self disappears, and 8) a sense of duration of time is altered.

In short, a state of flow keeps you occupied enough that you lose the sense of time, don't get tired and nothing else seems to matter. Your zone of influence is thoroughly claimed by your zone of concern. Or, as Robin Sharma puts it, 'Being engaged in a pursuit that truly challenges you is the surest route to personal satisfaction.'[9]

Now, here is the key question: On a typical work day, where do you find yourself mostly: anxiety or boredom? I suspect it is largely boredom, punctuated by spikes of anxiety. You oscillate between boredom and anxiety, without giving yourself sufficient time to be in the flow channel. The flow happens when you pick up a challenge and then develop skills to overcome the challenge, and before you risk getting bored again, you up the ante by picking up another challenge. Alternatively, if you have developed a skill then get cracking on a task that puts your skill to test, and then spiral outwards from there.

While working at the SLV-3 (Satellite Launch Vehicle) project at ISRO in late 1979, A.P.J. Abdul Kalam was in that flow channel which he called 'moments of magic'. He wrote in his memoir, *The Wings of Fire*, 'Although we were working very hard we were very relaxed, energetic and fresh . . . Perhaps it was the meaningful organization of the purposes we sought to achieve.' He incisively declared, 'Flow is the by-product of controlled creativity.'[10]

The flow is your calling in life. For me, it is reading, writing and teaching. I literally lose all sense of time while doing any of these. I feel complete, alive, relevant, refreshed and, above all, purposeful. I am living in the present. Now I understand what Krishnamurti meant when he said, 'Living in the present is the instant perception of beauty and the great delight in it without seeking pleasure from it.'[11] The flow itself is pleasurable, and not what it brings about.

What's the best analogy to flow? Water. And this is what a major proponent of flow, Bruce Lee, offered:[12]

> Be like water; water has form and yet it has no form. It is the softest element on earth, yet it penetrates the hardest rock. It has no shape of its own, yet it can take any shape in which it is placed. In a cup, it becomes the shape of the cup. In a vase, it takes the shape of the vase and curls about the stems of flowers. Put it in a teapot, it becomes the teapot. Please observe the adaptability of water. If you squeeze it fast, the water will flow out quickly. If you squeeze it slowly, it will come out slowly. Water may seem to move in contradiction, even uphill, but it chooses any way open to it so that it may reach the sea. It may flow swiftly or it may flow slowly, but its purpose is inexorable, its destiny sure.

Be like water. Always in a state of flow. And for what you don't flow with, let others take it up.

Delegate with confidence

Through my years of teaching and coaching, I have come across hundreds of managers and even a few leaders, and I often ask them this question: When you delegate, what is your objective: 1) getting the work done as per your expectations, or 2) getting the work done? Most managers go with the first option, whereas leaders settle with the 'work done'. There is little doubt they are there for a reason.

Effective delegation is the sine qua non of leadership. If you struggle in delegation, not only that do you not allow people below you or around you to grow, but you also sever your own growth prospects. Let's do a thought experiment to understand this better.

Suppose there are five CXOs reporting to a CEO. These are chiefs of marketing, sales, human resources, finance and production. The most suitable of them is the Chief Marketing Officer (CMO). He is so good that there's nobody even 70 per cent as efficient as him in his team. So, who do you think will be the next CEO? I can bet that it won't be our vastly talented CMO, for he has no one fitting in his shoes. By not delegating effectively and not preparing his next rung, he is not only truncating others' growth but also jeopardizing his own, notwithstanding his personal excellence. Hope you are not that manager!

The veteran US Navy SEAL officer Jocko Willink deems that pushing decision-making down to the subordinate, front-line leaders is critical to the success of any mission. As a leader, you must be adept at communicating up and down the line of command, effortlessly. As long as those reporting to you aren't fully into the mission, they can't operate freely, as was seen with the frozen Soviet Army as it was attacked by the Germans in 1941. The soldiers were awaiting orders from Moscow and didn't act on the imminent threat lest they earn the wrath of Stalin. It was thanks to the harsh winters that the Germans retreated, or else the fate of WW II would have been very different. Decentralization of decision-making is crucial under uncertainty—whether posed by the business environment, or the fog of war.

'Proper Decentralized Command requires simple, clear, concise orders that can be understood easily by everyone in the chain of command,' writes Willink in his book, *Extreme Ownership*. 'With clear guidance and established boundaries for decision-making that your subordinate leaders understand, they can then act independently toward your unified goal.' Delegate not just tactical matters but also planning, for often those at the periphery have more prior and acute knowledge about external developments. This frees you up to take bigger and more distant engagements. But in the interim, notes Willink, you must 're-examine what you can do to better clarify, educate, influence, or convince that person to give you what you need in order to win.'[13]

The art and science of delegation is as critical for the first-time managers as it is to the entrepreneurs, for you can go only so far riding on your personal calibre. And frankly, why are you the most suitable? You ought to give others a chance. That's your *Employees Quadrant* (refer to Figure 9). Most employees get delegated to. So, here we look at how to delegate effectively.

If we revisit the Urgency-Importance matrix, delegation is a matter of the third quadrant.

If you realize something is not important for you personally but is urgent for the system, you must delegate the task. There could be three types of delegation: upward, sideward and downward. Let's revisit the question: What would you want? —1) getting the work done as per your expectations, or 2) getting the work done? If you think the work must be done as per your standards, then you are mistaken on prioritization. If it must be done to your standards, then you better do it yourself. If you are choosing to delegate, make the standards impersonal.

Imagine you delegate 100 per cent of an activity to somebody, then how much of your time is freed up? A 100 per cent, pertaining to that activity. And what do you do with that time? You perform disciplined execution of things that matter to you or invest in high-leverage activities. Most people fail to delegate not because of distrust in others, but because they don't know what to do with their freed up time. Ergo, they remain parasitic to their work.

Some rules of delegation:

Direction is 80 per cent casting

In the entertainment industry, it's often said that direction is 80 per cent casting. Some say it's even 90 per cent! However, there is no denying the fact that if you get the right actor for the role, more than half of your task as a leader is achieved. The same applies to organizations: Getting the right people in the bus and on the right seats, and wrong people off the bus before you start. You can't argue about 'which way', once you start the bus. As most leaders admit, a majority of their time is spent in mapping right roles to appropriate people and then doing whatever is possible to enable them to perform those roles. If you mess that up, you end up spending a lot of time micromanaging others, and almost doing their job.

When asked about how the middle management shapes organizational culture, Satya Nadella is quick to note, 'Your job is to find the rose petals in a field of shit.'[14] It is to bring clarity to those who work with you, inspire them with palpable energy, and find a way to deliver success. It is to make the call, but not always expect the consensus. Some will align, and yet others won't. But be clear that for those who don't align, they must move on, however senior they may be. Nadella asked a few of his very senior leaders to leave the company when he realized that they weren't a part of the shared vision. That calls for courage.

70 per cent and go . . .

Who should be the right person for the task? Should the person be 100 per cent ready? No. Just settle for 70 per cent readiness. When is the person 100 per cent ready? Only on the job. Were you 100 per cent ready before you took up yours? Never. You learnt most of it along the way. In fact, there is a large tacit portion of knowledge, or the 'know how', apart from the explicit component, the 'know what', that you learn only once you start performing the job. Is it possible that somebody who is 70 per cent of you can become 120 per cent of you in due time? Yes, very much. You need to give them a chance.

In fact, a good marker of succession planning is how many people in your team are 70 per cent of you, in terms of job readiness. Don't fear such people. They are your passport to higher planes.

Take your hands off, but never your eyes off

Let's talk about the thorny issue of micromanagement, which infests almost all forms of delegation. Since you 'know' what's best, you tend to direct the proceedings, thereby depriving everyone of learning and development, yourself included. Instead, take your hands off, and let the person own the task, entirely. Only then is there skin in the game. If you are at standby, the other person will never be committed fully.

But be careful not to take your eyes off the person. Always keep watching them from the corner of your eye. If the other person doesn't see that you are keeping an eye, they will consider that the task doesn't matter; moreover, that *they* don't matter. When you teach your child bicycling, you need to leave them alone to balance themselves, but when they fall, they will want to see you rushing towards them.

Show the big picture, and cut them loose

Why will somebody consider working on a task which you think is unimportant for you? You need to create a serious reason for the other person, and an enduring one at that. That's where purpose is vital. You must keep the purpose consistent and the progress (towards it) visible. It's critical that the person knows what she's working towards and how her little efforts move the needle. It can do wonders. It's imperative to be clear about the 'why' and the 'what', but you must leave the 'how' ambiguous.

If you become too descriptive about how exactly a task needs to be performed, you are practically sapping away all creative juices off your team. They are just highly paid bots. As General George Patton would instruct us: Don't tell people how to do things; tell them what to do and let them surprise you with their results.

Learn to kill your habits

How about the tasks which are neither valuable to you nor to the system, and yet you carry on with those out of sheer habit? First thing in the morning, you check all your mails; you dutifully wish strangers on their birthdays; you never miss the 10:30 a.m. gossip round with your team, and then another one at 4:30 p.m.; you feel morally wrong in logging out of a meeting lest your boss makes a move, and the list goes on. These are all thoughtless activities that you have never got to question.

With so much technology at your disposal, you must bring it to bearing. Why not cut down on activities which are not valuable to you anymore, or to others. There are tasks which are not even worth delegating. They must be done away with, brutally. For the rest, automate, as much as possible. Free up your plate. Only then can you pick up other high-leverage activities. You must critically examine your day and what all you are busy with, and operate on your calendar with a surgical knife. Kill your habits, for all habits are bad. That's your *Technology Quadrant*.

Where do you start from: 1, 2, 3 or 4? I reckon, you start with 4, the 'Kill your Habits' quadrant, and you generously use technology there. Technology is an obedient slave, but a tyrant master. If you use it well, you are on top of the game, but if you allow it, or others with it, to use you, then you are doomed.

You move from 4 to 2 to 1 to 3. Free up the plate, plant high-leverage activities, execute them with discipline, and pass them on to others so that you can move further. Further, to solve important problems.

Solve important problems permanently

The human mind is essentially a problem-solving device. You are sitting in a comfortable setting, feeling secure because our ancestors were adept at solving problems right in the middle of the savannah, fending off saber-tooth tigers. No fancy stuff, just problem-solving, for what can be dearer than your very life. If you observe carefully, you are solving countless problems on a daily basis—some very well, others not so much—but you get past problems, anyhow. Our brain is designed to solve problems related to surviving in an unstable outdoor environment, and to do so in nearly constant motion. And yet, we all differ widely in our problem-solving abilities. Some embrace it willingly while others despise it.

An important problem solved permanently can make you immortal (well, almost). Those who conserve and converge their attention on to significant issues get their names etched in the annals of time. 'Ever since I was told by some of the greatest men of the time, leaders in science whose names are immortal, that I am possessed of an unusual mind, I bent all my thinking faculties on the solution of great problems regardless of sacrifice,' noted Tesla.[15] Tesla, along with Edison, was of that kind. Lincoln, Gandhi, Mandela and Martin Luther all solved a different set of important problems.

Let's get to how to solve important problems well.

As you have learned from hindsight, or so I assume, that not every problem is worth solving, even if it looks alarming at that moment. Think of two types of problems: 1) a *bruise* that gets healed over time, and 2) a *cancer* that worsens over time. A bruise might hurt you then, but whether you apply an ointment or put a bandage, it won't significantly alter the course of its healing. Even if it's left to its own devices, nature will take care of it (in most cases). Whereas a tumour, even though benign, will certainly grow malign if not addressed in time. So, the effect of time on the two types of problems is dramatically different; it solves one, it aggravates the other. Your genius is in identifying the right one and then rationing your attention and efforts accordingly.

In a corporate milieu, or even in life, in general, which one do you think forms the giant share of problems: bruises or cancerous growth? I guess, it's bruises. No more than 20 per cent of all the problems can you classify as cancer. With consciousness and by reflecting on your experiences, you can hone heuristics to distil the problems with greater accuracy. Time is of essence here. And brilliance is in differentiating a painful bruise from a fatal cancer, and acting accordingly.

Equally important is the impact of the problem. A good question to ask is: Does it bother my boss's boss? You may be busy solving numerous problems daily, but very few have a significant impact. If a problem, whether ignored or solved very well, doesn't impact those who are two levels above you, it's not worth it. The consulting firm McKinsey has a useful heuristic here: 'Don't solve a problem that doesn't bother the client's CEO.' I guess, that's a powerful way of putting a premium on your efforts.

As shown in Figure 11, every time you encounter a problem, ask yourself two questions: 1) What will happen to this problem over time: will it get diluted or aggravated; and 2) Will it bother my boss's boss. If the problem is serious and of high stakes, take time to address it.

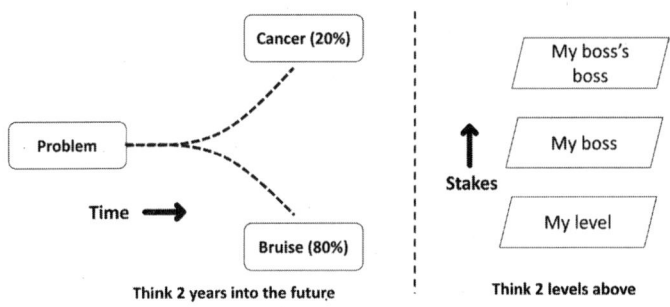

Figure 11: How to prioritize problems.

Putting together the factors of time and impact, I propose:

Conjecture #1: Just because you can (solve a problem) doesn't mean you should.

In fact, expert problem-solvers spend considerable time selecting the problem before applying themselves to it. It is especially important in an uncertain context, where you don't have a surefire approach to solve a problem. The more complex the setting, the greater is the importance of going slow and being selective. The context defines the efforts you put in picking up a problem and the approach to solving it. 'Kind learning environment experts choose a strategy and then evaluate; experts in less repetitive environments evaluate and then choose,' notes David Epstein.[16] The former is a chess match, while the latter is a game of poker. And most of life is poker.

Now, let's understand how we confuse mere symptoms with problems. Suppose you visit a doctor and she asks you: 'So, tell me your problem?' You start rattling off, 'I have a sore throat, a running nose. I have lost my appetite, I feel weak all day long, etc.' What are you narrating: problems or symptoms? I guess, it's symptoms. The doctor categorically asked you your problems and yet you chose the vocabulary of symptoms. Why? Is it that you want to hide something from the doctor, or mislead her? Or you don't really know what's ailing you? Most likely you have no idea what's ailing you and yet you have the audacity to *know* others' problems.

What you know of others are mere symptoms and not the actual problem, let alone the root causes. Calling a mere symptom a problem can be a gross mistake, for you will mostly come up with superficial fixes. Does calling a phenomenon a problem versus a symptom really make any difference? Let's see. If I call attrition a problem versus a symptom, how does your approach change? If you think of it as a problem you tend to solve it, and resort to the old, time-tested solutions; whereas if you think of it as a symptom you tend to diagnose it and, hopefully, create new solutions.

Hence, my second proposition is:

Conjecture #2: Every problem is a mere symptom.

We generally tend to think in exact opposite terms. We think of symptoms as real problems, and attack those, prematurely. Consequently, we tend to solve the problems partially, if not aggravating those further. Can we solve important problems permanently? Is there a method to it? Yes, there is. Let's delve deeper.

Every time you encounter a symptom (disguised as a problem), you have two choices: to solve it readily, or to investigate it further. In most circumstances, you will tend to solve the symptom—the reason being that you don't have sufficient time and resources. Let's call that approach 'Quick Fix'.

Most managers are competent at quick fixes, as it keeps them in their jobs. A Quik Fix is also known as jugaad.

But if the symptom is recurring and serious, you will want to investigate further and get to the underlying problems. For instance, some of the known causes of high employee turnover are poor work environment, demotivating supervisors, inadequate compensation and a meaningless job, among others. But should you stop at that? If you can go one level further and get to the root causes, then you are more likely to solve the problem permanently. The key operative here is 'root causes' and not root cause. You must be comfortable with the idea that there are a bunch of causes that work in concert and that addressing just one or few of those won't move the needle significantly. This requires patience and prudence—to go all the way through and prioritize the most serious of the root causes (you can adopt the heuristics discussed in Figure 11). This approach of solutioning for the important root causes is 'Perma Fix', short for permanent fix. The approach is shown in Figure 12.

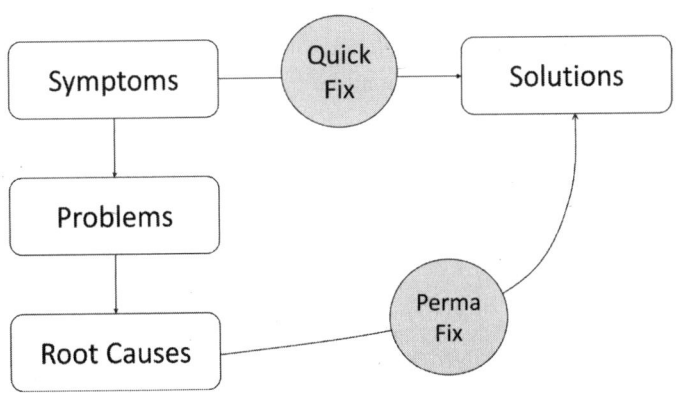

Figure 12: An approach to solving problems permanently.

As an analogy, problem-solving is like sculpting. Where is the sculpture? It is hidden right inside the stone. The craft is to chisel out the stone so that the creation is revealed, one stroke at a time. Similarly, where is the solution? Hidden right inside the problem. It takes disciplined chiselling to reveal the solution in its full glory. The key is to go beyond the broad contours to the finer details.

This takes me to the last and probably the most important proposition.

Conjecture #3: A problem fully understood is half solved.

Most people don't put in the effort to understand the problem fully, as they are grappling with too many problems (read symptoms). That's where Perma Fix is a very important tool in your arsenal.

Generally, you will address almost 70 per cent of the problems in a Quick Fix manner, and 30 per cent in a Perma Fix way. This may change as you progress. It's because not every problem is worth delving deeper into (Conjecture #1), and, further, Perma Fix is resource-consuming. When should you resort to Quick Fix and when to go for the Perma Fix? Here's some assistance.

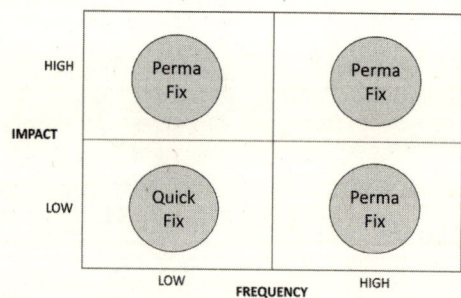

Figure 13: Choice of Perma Fix versus Quick Fix.

If you plot the problems on to a 2x2 of Impact and Frequency, you will get to four quadrants. Problems with low impact and low frequency, such as rare absenteeism of employees, could be dealt with a Quick Fix. The high impact, low frequency problems, such as a rare misconduct with a female employee, should need a Perma Fix. Similarly, a low impact, high frequency problem, such as wastage of food at the cafeteria, also calls for a Perma Fix. And very likely, a high impact and high frequency problem, such as consistent low ratings on employee satisfaction, necessitates a Perma Fix. If you start to plot your problem on this simple 2x2, it will certainly help you prioritize better.

Nothing offers greater self-confidence than a difficult problem solved permanently. At a metaphysical level, M. Scott Peck offers, 'Problems do not go away. They must be worked through or else they remain, forever a barrier to the growth and development of the spirit.'[17] Resonated Eckhart, 'When survival is threatened by seemingly unsurmountable problems, an individual life-form—or a species—will either die or become extinct or rise above the limitations of its condition through an evolutionary leap.'[18] Learning to solve wicked problems well is that evolutionary leap.

In nineteenth century England, cholera was a major cause of death. Between 1848 and 1854, a series of cholera outbreaks rocked London, resulting in thousands of deaths. The situation was so severe that in one week during September 1854, over 600 deaths were reported, primarily in the Soho area adjacent to Broad Street. The prevailing paradigm at that time was 'Miasma Theory', which attributed cholera to the airborne transmission of poisonous vapours emerging from the foul smells due to poor sanitation, in this case the overflowing Thames River.

John Snow, a physician and the personal anaesthetist to Queen Victoria, took it upon himself to systematically investigate the cause of deaths. Ruling out the Miasma Theory, Snow meticulously traced all the deaths to a single source of water: the Broad Street pump.

Snow, the father of modern epidemiology, described his reasoning as follows:[19]

> I found that nearly all the deaths had taken place within a short distance of the pump . . . there were sixty-one instances in which I was informed that the deceased persons used to drink the water from Broad Street, either constantly or occasionally . . .
>
> The Workhouse in Poland Street is more than three-quarters surrounded by houses in which deaths from cholera occurred, yet out of five hundred and thirty-five inmates, only five died of cholera . . . The Workhouse has a pump-well on the premises, in addition to the supply from the Grand Junction Waterworks, and the inmates never sent to the Broad Street for water. If the mortality in the Workhouse had been equal to that in the streets immediately surrounding it . . . upward of one hundred persons would have died.
>
> The result of the inquiry then was that there has been no particular outbreak or increase of cholera, in this part of London, except among the persons who were in the habit of drinking water of the above-mentioned pump-well.

Arriving at the suspect, Snow persuaded the reluctant civic authorities to remove the handle of the Broad Street pump, and, within days, the cholera was gone.

Symptom: large-scale cholera-related deaths in an isolated community; Problem: a specific pump in a specific locality; Root Cause: people consuming contaminated water; Solution: remove the handle of the pump. Can you think of a cheaper solution for avoiding deaths? Once problems are fully understood, the solutions are staring right at you. (Ignaz Semmelweis comes to mind here.)

So, the next time you are confronted with a problem, you should take time to assess it, be critical in framing it, and thorough in solving it. But never forget to sell your solutions.

Tell stories without ppts

'Humans think in stories rather than in facts, numbers or equations, and the simpler the story, the better,' notes Yuval Noah Harari. 'Human groups are defined more by the changes they undergo than by any continuity, but they nevertheless manage to create for themselves ancient identities thanks to their storytelling skills.'[20] Ergo, in the world of big data, cold analytics, machine learning and general-purpose artificial intelligence, the premium is back on prose and poetry. When you are bombarded with massive amounts of information, mostly uninvited, what sticks are stories.

Bill Clinton, the forty-second President of the US, attributes his success in politics to his upbringing when there was no television. He was raised at a time where you were either narrating stories or listening to them.[21] And that's a skill the following generation of leaders have not kept up with. 'A Place Called Hope' is a story that's worth retelling and there are few storytellers better than Clinton.

What's the deal with stories? All stories have emotions, and as it turns out, emotionally charged events are better remembered—whether they are facts or fictions. When your brain detects an emotionally charged event, your amygdala releases dopamine into your bloodstream which enhances your memory and information processing capacity. You don't even have to experience the event; you can simply imagine it, as being told through a story.

Stories can move people and that's why we still watch movies, read novels and indulge in gossip. Annette Simmons, a community activist and an organizational coach, identifies six types of stories that we typically hear or narrate: 1) 'Who I Am' stories; 2) 'Why I Am Here' stories; 3) 'The Vision' stories; 4) 'Teaching' stories; 5) 'Values in Action' stories; and 6) 'I Know What You Are Thinking' stories. Unlike the naked truth, Annette opines, 'Story is less direct, more gracious, and prompts less resistance.'[22] Try one of these for yourself in your next client or team meeting (start with 'The Vision' story).

But beware of cheap talk. Cheap talk, or small talk, is the downside of storytelling. You don't even know in your well-woven narrative when you have lost contact with the ground. And it doesn't take much for others to see through your fluff. As the saying goes in the investment circuit: *Don't tell me what you think, tell me what you have in your portfolio.* Which again goes back to having a skin in the game and to maintaining a knowledge differential.

One useful advice is to back your assertions with solid evidence and data. A go-to tool here is Barbara Minto's *Pyramid Principle*.[23] As the first female MBA professional hired by McKinsey, Barbara served the firm between 1963 and 1973 and has devised some incisive frameworks of thinking coherently and communicating clearly.

The Pyramid Principle states that a recommendation must be backed by supporting arguments which, in turn, are built on data. This layered style of communication is very effective, for it not only offers you clarity while thinking and writing, but also helps your audience consume information more readily, without the risk of alienating or inundating them. 'The great value of the technique,' notes Barbara, 'is that it forces you to pull out of your head information that you weren't aware was there, and then helps you to develop and shape it until the thinking is crystal clear.'[24]

A useful heuristic is to keep such arguments or data points mutually exclusive and collectively exhaustive, aka MECE (pronounced as mee-cee), another enduring contribution by Barbara. You ensure that your communication offers maximum coverage with minimum text. Hence, you structure your sentences, bullet points and arguments in a mutually exclusive category to ensure minimum redundancy or overlap, and yet cover all the key content, whereby ensuring they are collectively exhaustive.

Not just your recommendations, but also the way you build up to those is very consequential. You follow the SCQA method. It starts by narrating the *Situation* so that your audience is up to speed on the context and is able to empathize with your agenda. Then you bring in the *Complication*, or the hook of your story, which demands attention and arouses curiosity. You thereafter state your core *Question*, which you have set out to address, and this is followed by the *Answer*, which is typically in a MECE format, not less than three and not more than five points. All of this takes you about two minutes and that's your elevator pitch.

Why does the elevator pitch work? It works because your brain always seeks meaning before details. Your resource-scarce, ever-optimizing brain latches on to the gist of a situation before moving to the more peripheral details, if necessary. If the gist is devoid of any meaning, details have no chance. Now think of the overworked mind of a senior executive or an investor. You need to make the most of the first ninety seconds. The details can always be parked for a later date, or for the juniors. Information, when presented in a hierarchical fashion, through a mind map or a logical pyramid, has greater chances of retention, as it offers high level details before moving to the nitty gritty.

Figure 14 depicts the Pyramid Principle, along with the elevator pitch technique of SCQA.

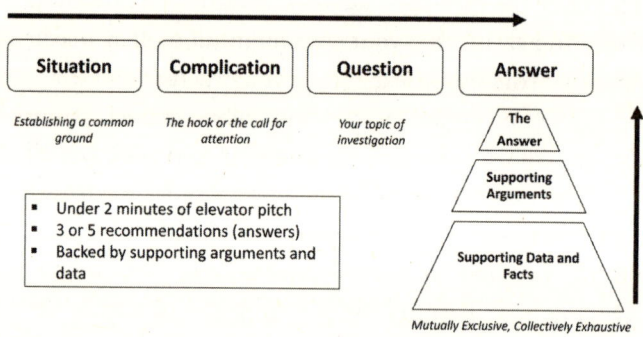

Figure 14: The Pyramid Principle explained, along with SCQA model of elevator pitch (Source: Barbara Minto).

Imagine you are in a conversation with a difficult customer, or with your hyperactive, attention deficit boss, and you have to convince your audience for another detailed meeting. You follow the Pyramid Principle of layered communication. If your recommendations are accepted as such, don't bother others with your arguments or data. If it must go to the arguments, still keep the data up your sleeve, and if you must, then only bare it all. Understand that not everyone has the appetite for dense data, especially the higher-ups. Unveil your arsenal on a necessity basis, but always keep it ready and rehearsed.

Needless to say that a good story must be simple. If you can't explain it in simple terms, you haven't understood it. 'The mark of genius is the capacity to see and to express what is simple, simply!', opined Bruce Lee.[25]

Now just go back to the previous passage. How shallow would have been my treatment of storytelling without the relevant references and some practical tools? That's what I meant by 'no cheap talk'. In fact, the entire book has been an attempt to keep the standards of conversation high, backed with rigorous research and anecdotal evidence. And that's perhaps why you have reached thus far.

Now, let's talk about being strategic.

5

Think Strategically, Act Decisively

'If you want to leave your footprints on the sands of time, do not drag your feet.'

—A.P.J. Kalam[1]

You may die accidentally, but you can't afford to live accidentally. Your plans do and will fail, but you can't afford to not plan. Keep in mind that plans do fail, but planning doesn't. Developing a strategic mindset is that planning skill—the ability to cut through the clutter to make sense for yourself and those around you.

When I ask people to hone a strategic mindset, most offer a rebuke, saying, 'I am not senior enough'. Point taken. But I am not talking about devising a strategy for your company; instead, I am talking about your life and career. Even if you don't own the fate of your company, you certainly do yours. Being a strategic thinker is for everyone, and not just for leaders. Even when you are following a well-laid-out strategy, you need to maintain clarity of thought and the ability to make high quality decisions with minimal information or guidance. Take, for instance, the military forces.

Let me take your memory to 18 September 2016. Four Jaish-e-Mohammed militants from Pakistan carried out an attack at the Indian Army Uri Brigade headquarters in Jammu and Kashmir, killing nineteen soldiers and injuring another two dozen. The martyrs were from the Army's 10th Battalion, Dogra Regiment, and 6th Battalion, Bihar Regiment. The nation was in shock, but also was by now numbed by the frequency and audacity of such skirmishes on the Line of Control (LoC) with Pakistan.

While the world knows what happened next, let's get into the behind the scenes stuff of the surgical strike.

India's Parachute Regiment SF (Special Forces) is trained for such operations: attack and destroy. Within days of the assault, three separate Ghatak teams were formed comprising SF and men from the Dogra 10 and Bihar 6, to avenge the killing of their brothers-in-arms. They were to cross the border from three different locations, with specific targets assigned to them.

The cheat sheet for the Ghatak platoons looked as follows. Column 1: name of the location to be attacked; Column 2: distance inside PaK (Pakistan-administered Kashmir) from the LoC; Column 3: number of terrorists hiding at each location; Column 4: details of men, equipment, logistics and backup support; and Column 5: number of casualties India may suffer at each location. The last column totalled to a double-digit number.[2]

Major Mike Tango was leading his Ghatak team of nineteen at Uri, waiting for the marching orders. His team was supposed to eliminate two of the four launch pads. While the team was equipped with M4A1 5.56 mm carbines, Tavor TAR-21 assault rifles, Instalaza C90 disposable grenade launchers, Galil sniper rifles and night vision equipment, the real risk was in the de-induction. It's on the return journey where Major Tango was suspecting maximum casualty. But he had to plan and take a chance.

Finally, on 27 September, the orders came to strike. Major Tango's team of Para-SF started at 8:30 p.m. that night. Their task was to eliminate two launch pads, roughly 500 metres away, cause maximum damage and get back to the Indian side of the border without losing a man. The team crossed across the border in the stealth of the night, waited an entire day while observing the activities of the terrorists, and then chose to strike the following night. Major Tango split his team into two, each carrying out the mission in complete radio silence, led from the front as he eliminated four terrorists in a close encounter, chose a quick exit out of the site while facing the full firepower of the Pakistan Army and not leaving a trace behind. The team crossed the LoC and came back at 4:30 a.m. on 29 September.

Twenty terrorists were eliminated in a fight that lasted less than an hour. Planning time: one week. Mission duration: thirty-six hours. Casualties on the Indian side (Column 5): zero. That is called honing a strategic mindset. To think the big picture, take a future-back approach, hone mental models on how to behave under stress, be willing to make trade-offs and always being a step ahead of the adversaries.

Let's delve deeper into these aspects.

Always think the big picture

Thinking the big picture doesn't come automatically. Most people would rather avoid tripping over at all costs, even if they are heading in the wrong direction. It's critical to lift your head once in a while, take stock of the situation, and ask yourself some vital questions.

Remember this: *The evolution of your thinking is not a natural consequence of your career progression.*

Just because you got promoted doesn't mean that your thinking also got promoted. Even at the height of the organizational totem pole, you may still be prone to rolling your sleeves and going after every problem that comes your way. If you can't take a strategic perspective—a long-term view of the problem—then no marks for solving it well. If the problem itself is not important, no amount of solutioning can elevate its status. No marks for hard work here.

A useful heuristic is to ask the 'so what' question. Who cares if the problem is not solved? What happens if it does get solved? Is the problem worth solving?

As shown in Figure 15, every time you encounter a problem, always ask two questions: 1) Why solve the problem, and 2) How to solve it. If you don't get a compelling answer to the first question and it doesn't take you to a higher plane, then don't bother about the second question. There are far more tools available for problem-solving than for problem validation, prioritization and articulation. Between identifying a problem and solving it, which one do you think can be delegated? Which one can be outsourced, or even automated? I reckon, it's the solutioning part that's more amicable to be pushed down or out. Which means your cognitive efforts must be pushed up, towards the big picture.

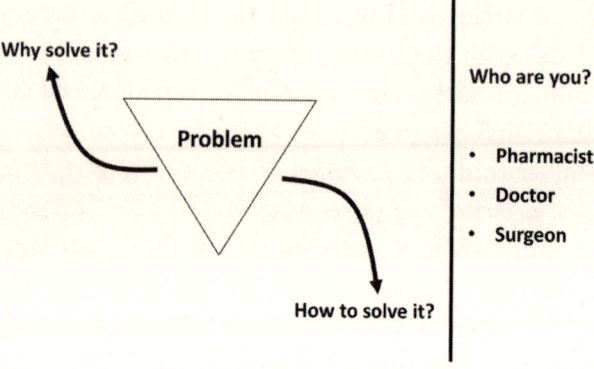

Figure 15: Taking the big picture view on every problem. Are you a pharmacist, doctor, or a surgeon?

The higher you go, the broader you must look; else your elevation has little significance for yourself, or even to those around you. You will see scores of managers busy reorganizing the chairs on the deck of the Titanic, not realizing that the whole enterprise is sinking! But since their job description narrowly demanded the chairs to be properly organized, they got trapped into it, and then the very job got obliterated. Whom to blame? No one but the self.

When a task is asked of you, you must always ask the ones in authority, or at least yourself, as to what's it leading to. If you fail to seek the big picture, you are doomed to be meaninglessly busy, chipping along an insignificant path. Often, asking such probing questions can be cathartic for those around or above you, but if you don't then you will never get to thinking any differently.

On why you must seek clarity from those above you, Jocko Willink advises, 'If you don't understand or believe in the decisions coming down from your leadership, it is up to you to ask questions until you understand how and why those decisions are being made.'[3] He further admits that it takes courage to knock at the CEO's door, but it invariably helps.

With respect to the level of thinking, we can identify three types of employees: pharmacist, doctor and surgeon. A pharmacist is an expert in giving you the medicine, as prescribed by the doctor. Apart from the skill of reading funny handwriting, the pharmacist is adept at matching the names to medicines and, in certain cases, offers you alternatives of similar salts. In rural settings, such pharmacists also double up as make-do doctors, offering drugs for common cough and cold. But they never bother about the big picture. Your particular ailment doesn't concern them. What happens after you ingest the medicine is the least of their concerns. They are experts at optimizing transactions. Such employees demand, 'Tell me what needs to be done, but don't bother me with details.' They remain right there, as expert troubleshooters.

Next comes the doctors. You walk up to a doctor with your unique symptoms (unique in your head) and the doctor excels at mapping your unique symptoms to commonly known problems and then matching those to commonly available solutions. She will seldom create a new solution for you. Her skills are to diagnose, with the help of a battery of tests, and offer you the best possible map. She cares about the big picture, as in your family history, previous encounters with similar problems, your diet, lifestyle, et al., but doesn't get into your skin. Once you walk out of the door, her skin in the game is once again zero. She's not as transactional as a pharmacist, and perhaps that's why you visit her again. She's like an employee who asks, 'Why should I solve this problem? Tell me more.' They can be annoying, but they often reveal the truth.

Finally, we have the surgeon. You walk up to a surgeon when not much has worked. After understanding your ailment, she devises a plan of action for you. Ask any surgeon if any two surgeries are similar and they will assure you that they are only as good as their last operation. A hundred things can go wrong in an OT. She has to not only understand you, your ailment, your history, but also keep a big picture view of what all can go wrong before, during and after the surgery. While she gets into your skin, literally, she maintains her skin in your life even after you are off the hook. Her knowledge asymmetry gives her the ability to handle your life, while you sign on the dotted line, taking full responsibility for what happens to you. She's like the employee who asks, 'Are we solving the right problem? What happens next? Let's explore.'

There are instances when solving a problem seems pressing, but the real deal is what happens once the problem is solved. Are you creating a bigger one? In medicine, it's quite natural to move from one ailing patient to the next, going about the motions, but a real surgeon maintains an elevated view, a humane disposition to fellow humans. His years of performing neurosurgery made Kalanithi reckon that 'The physician's duty is not to stave off death or return patients to their old lives, but to take into our arms a patient and family whose lives have disintegrated and work until they can stand back up and face, and make sense of, their own existence.'[4]

At an uber level, India's foreign policy is testimony to big picture thinking. For a long time, India's disposition to the world was largely dictated by others. Initially by the USA and Soviet Union, and later by the European Union and China. Lately, India is flexing its muscles in a multi-polar world and creating its own space, backed by its economic heft and cultural soft power. Take, for instance, the Russia-Ukraine war that began in February 2022. India was under enormous pressure from the West to sever its ties with Russia and issue stern statements at the United Nations and elsewhere, reprimanding India's former ally for its aggression. Our leadership didn't buckle under pressure. We continued ties with Russia, while making inroads into the Western hegemony. If anything, India took the crucial role of bringing the two adversaries to a common table. Ditto with the Israel-Hamas conflict, where while India stands with Israel and against terrorism, there is no going back on the humanitarian aid India continues to provide to Palestine and elsewhere in the Middle East.

On assuming the Presidency of the G20, India dealt with several tricky issues with finesse and in time, without giving away its self-interest. Under the stewardship of the likes of Amitabh Kant, the G20 Sherpa, Subrahmanyam Jaishankar, India's External Affairs Minister, Piyush Goyal, Trade Minister, and other tough negotiators, India emerged as a 'third option'. By incorporating the African Union into the venerated G20, India has cemented its position as a representative of the Global South, the bulwark against Chinese aggression, and counterbalance to the wild West.

'This is a time for us to engage America, manage China, cultivate Europe, reassure Russia, bring Japan into play, draw neighbours in, extend the neighbourhood and expand traditional constituencies of support,' writes Jaishankar. 'Our approach should be to build comfort with the world, not opaqueness or distance. There will be a natural suspicion of all rising powers that we will have to allay. Taking on global responsibilities, acting as a constructive player and projecting our own distinct personality are elements of that solution. India is better off being liked than just being respected.'[5]

This is big picture thinking. India's leadership is acting like a surgeon (remember the surgical strike?).

So, who are you—pharmacist, doctor or surgeon? All three survive, but you know their relative value to the customer and in society. If you maintain a big picture view, you get richly rewarded. But it takes discipline. Here's another aspect on how to maintain a strategic perspective:

Think future-back and outside-in

Suppose you want to be an entrepreneur in the next five years, which of the two approaches will you choose: A) You think five years out and identify the practices you must start, stop and sustain beginning today to realize the desired outcome; or B) You continue doing your best today and hope that you will achieve the prized outcome? I deem that you will choose option A. Option B may make you feel comfortable, and you may still reach somewhere but not necessarily the entrepreneur position that you so much desired. And yet most of us tread path B, for we know no better.

How about adopting a future-back thinking, instead of the usual present-forward approach? 'Prediction,' as goes the old proverb, 'is hazardous, especially about the future.' And we experienced it first-hand. We had no clue towards the end of the year 2019 as to what was coming up in 2020, and even when we were staring at the worst-case scenario, very few predicted that most of us would be back to our usual selves in less than eighteen months, all inoculated. So, sitting today, what can I say about the future?

However, you can give yourself a goal and work backwards from it. It's a more deterministic approach than merely trusting your good fortune. As depicted in Figure 16, a future-back approach is about deciding what to: 1) *start* doing today that will take you closer to the desired outcome; 2) entirely *stop* doing, for it doesn't help or is outright counterproductive; and 3) *sustain* that is going right and is helping the cause. Which one do you think is the most difficult to articulate: start, stop or sustain? My experience tells me that it's 'stop'. Stopping what seems to be working well or even otherwise, isn't trivial. It calls for character.

Present-forward thinking hinges on a 'hope' that you will reach your destiny, whereas a future-back attitude is propelled by the 'willingness' to make it happen. In either case, you can fail. But in the future-back approach you know what didn't work, while in the present-forward model you will always wish that you worked harder.

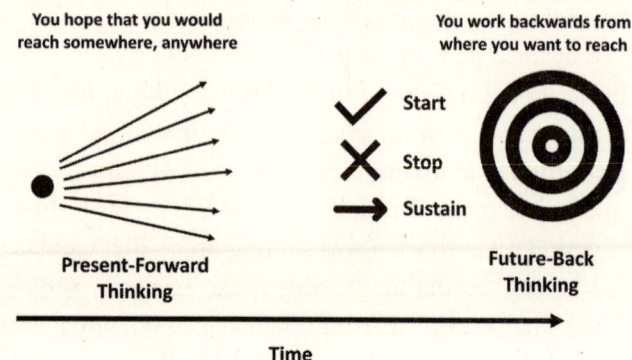

You hope that you would reach somewhere, anywhere

You work backwards from where you want to reach

Start

Stop

Sustain

Present-Forward Thinking

Future-Back Thinking

Time

Figure 16: Future-Back Thinking versus Present-Forward Thinking.

The start-stop-sustain, or the '3-S Model', can be applied to any situation. Suppose you wish to become a better parent; just write down three points under each action class and you are somewhat sorted. Then it's up to your discipline of execution. However, you must ascertain your goal first, and I would rather have one which is stretched, than a linear extrapolation of my present self.

Being clear with the end state and aware of your choice set is vital in life and business. A game which is deemed closest to the world of strategy is chess. Often, chess players are touted to be great strategists. But, as admits the five-time World Chess Champion, Viswanathan Anand, 'Many of the most beautiful games I've played have come about at a time when I knew very little and had just one strategic theme or a clear goal I was aiming to achieve.'[6] Too many things in his mind and the man can't operate. That's why future-back thinking.

The corollary to future-back thinking is outside-in thinking.

Answer this: What are you more acutely aware of—things which are happening inside your company, or the actions transpiring outside your company? I guess, you are more clued to the internal whereabouts than external intelligence. And I have little doubt you are always nastily surprised by external events, for you have little control over those. Disruptions almost always hit you from elsewhere, while you are busy organizing your shop. And that's what the legendary GE CEO Jack Welch said: 'If the rate of change on the outside exceeds the rate of change on the inside, the end is near.' This ultimatum is not just for leaders, but for each one of us.

The world around us is replete with opportunities and threats, or more generally speaking, trends, and if you are tuned into the external movements, you will be more likely to pivot before you are forced to. And yet most executives, and even entrepreneurs, remain busy taming the internal mess, as if operational efficiencies can somehow compensate for a lack of directional clarity. An external intelligence, almost in the manner of natural selection, dictates what's worth internally. If your organizational resources and competencies aren't valuable in the external context, they are mere liabilities. Think of the fate of office rentals when people migrated to working from home, or the way OTT platforms have run into movie theatres, threatening the once fledging industry.

Putting it back together, the ability to think future-back requires you to be acutely in tune with your external environment and operating context. An inside-out approach offers more weightage to what you have internally, whereas an outside-in stance attempts to leverage the external changes and is willing to modulate (through start, stop, sustain) what you have. It is a sobering thought that your strengths and weaknesses are only so in the context of your external reality.

It's not easy to foresee or to make sense of technology trends, and you may end up betting on wrong trajectories, as was the case of Microsoft with mobile phones, Google with social networks, and Amazon with a search engine. But a leader must, nonetheless, learn to call the shots amid the haze of uncertainty. 'A leader has to have an idea of what to do to innovate in the face of fear and inertia,' notes Satya Nadella. 'We need to be willing to lean into uncertainty, to take risks, and to move quickly when we make mistakes, recognizing failure happens along the way to mastery.'[7] That's your ability to overcome the sunk cost fallacy.

The capacity to envisage a future state and then steer the organization towards it through a difficult phase of metamorphosis is the hallmark of transformational leadership. Louis Gerstner, the former IBM chief and a rank outsider, could rescue the company from the jaws of death because he was willing to stop what worked so well in the 1970s and 1980s, but not anymore. He kept an eye on the future and an ear to the ground—listening to the customers, feeling the pulse of the employees, comprehending largescale technological and market shifts—and making some bold decisions. And when asked about his plan, Gerstner famously retorted, 'The last thing IBM needs right now is a vision.'[8]

Back home, we have the Captain Cool: M.S. Dhoni. In preparation for the inaugural T20 World Cup in 2007, one of the wild cards was the bowl-out. Introduced for the first time in cricket, this tiebreaker involves bowling at stumps and whichever team gets the most opponents to the cleaners will win. This rule has since then been modified numerous times. As a captain,

Dhoni had no reference or guidance for bowl-outs, but he had the innate ability to anticipate. Dhoni would start every practice session with bowl-outs and every player would give it a go, and whoever got maximum hits would bowl in the real tiebreaker.[9]

And so when India faced Pakistan in the defining qualifier on 14 September 2007, the successful bowlers for India were Virender Sehwag and Robin Uthappa, and not the front-liners. The fateful decision of giving the last over in the finals to the medium-pacer Joginder Sharma was another instance of outside-in and a future-back thinking by Dhoni. Sharma's poker face and non-threatening image made the opposition complacent, leading to errors of judgement, much in the favour of India. Where did this skill come from?

Of the several exploits the man from hinterland India has had on the international stage, one of the underlying traits has been Dhoni's uncanny ability to be situationally aware, aka 'street smartness'. His close aids, of whom there are not many, swear by his observational skills, that nothing misses his eyes. Was Dhoni always like that or did situations play a role here too? As it seems, the ability to spot, both people and opportunities, came from adversities.

While playing at Ranchi's MECON stadium, the young Dhoni was confronted with a stony turf and a rather punishing ball. So narrates his coach, Keshav Ranjan Banerjee, 'There are small and big stones on that ground. There was no point in removing all the stones; it would have taken forever. So, we would put a mat on top of those stones and play. You could never be sure how the ball would behave. One would come to your ankles while the next would fly past your ear.'[10] And, hence, were born the powerful pull shots that paid little respect to the ball or the baller.

Dhoni could traverse seamlessly between shot selection and player selection. That's big picture thinking, coupled with an ability to read the room, and a deftness in decision-making.

Closing this section with somebody who personifies a future-back and outside-in thinking: Astronaut José Hernández. Born to a Mexican immigrant, Hernández would spend half the year as a labourer in the fields of California and the rest in La Piedad, Mexico. Till the age of twelve, he didn't know English and yet harboured the dream of being an astronaut at NASA, inspired by the Apollo 17 mission of 1972. His migratory life never allowed him to continue his schooling properly. 'Honestly, life was hard because we would go to school Monday through Friday, but on Saturdays and Sundays we were working in the fields with our parents, and while our friends loved summer vacations, we hated them because that meant seven days of the week [working] in the fields,' recollects Hernández.

But his interest in Maths and Science prevailed and he went on to become a first-generation college student. After securing an M.S. in Electrical and Computer Engineering from UC Santa Barbara, Hernández applied to NASA. He was solemnly rejected. And then eleven more rejections followed. But every time he was declined an offer, he questioned himself on what he lacked. 'I started to look at the skills that the selected astronauts had and that I didn't.'[11] He took an outside-in approach: what others have, and I don't. A future-back approach: where I want to reach, and what I must start, stop and sustain to reach there.

Hernández learnt to be a fighter pilot and a deep-sea diver, clocking requisite hours of training, picked up the Russian language and anything that got him closer to those who got picked by NASA. Finally, in 2004, on his twelfth attempt, Hernández was selected, becoming the first Mexican astronaut, and was later assigned to the crew of Space Shuttle mission STS-128. His planning and perseverance prevailed. 'It's worth dreaming big when you are willing to put in the work that is needed to accomplish the goal you have,' Hernández believes. 'Obviously, the more difficult the goal, the more you will have to work . . . but everything is possible, and you should dare to dream big.'

If Dhoni and Hernández can reach to the very top of their professions, so can you. But by design. Dream big, read a lot, anticipate the future, put in your plan, back it with hard work and make it happen. But you need some tools by your side. Let's see a few important ones.

Construct proprietary mental models

Mental models are thinking shortcuts, or rules of thumb, that help you think clearly under uncertainty, or when you are inundated with too much information and have little time to make choices. Such models help reduce the data, insights, intuition, gut feel and other kinds of information into understandable and organizable chunks that speed up decision-making. These are derived from years of practice, experimentation and from situations where you have gone wrong.

Most leaders, that I have known or read about, have their own mental models or heuristics that they rely on to navigate through their lives and careers. The 'Two-Pizza Teams' is the mental model for Jeff Bezos; the 'Circle of Competence' is that of Warren Buffet; 'Buy it low, stake it high, sell it cheap' drove Sam Walton; 'Thought Experiments' is what Einstein adopted to build his theories; 'First Principles Thinking' is how Elon Musk goes about problem-solving; while Steve Jobs was famous for 'Via Negativa' (subtracting instead of adding).

On the importance of mental models, the famous investor Charlie Munger offers:[12]

> Well, the first rule is that you can't really know anything if you just remember isolated facts and try and bang 'em back. If the facts don't hang together on a latticework of theory, you don't have them in a usable form. You've got to have models in your head. And you've got to array your experience both vicarious and direct on this latticework of models. You may have noticed students who just try to remember and pound back what is remembered. Well, they fail in school and in life. You've got to hang experience on a latticework of models in your head.

While the psychologist and Nobel laureate Daniel Kahneman maintains that heuristics and mental shortcuts often lead to predictable biases and errors, the benefits far outstrip the costs when you are dealing with a familiar situation. You don't really want to go back to thinking from the very basics, given every problem or a situation. Mental models serve two key functions. Firstly, they save time and other critical resources, which are at a premium when you become more pivotal in the overall scheme of things. When the impact of your decisions, either way, right or wrong, is very high. Secondly, it saves you from the guilt of having made a rash decision. If you go wrong, you can always get back to tweaking your mental model, but at least you have something working instead of shooting blind. And so goes the saying: Good judgement comes from experience; experience comes from bad judgement.

Here's a useful mental model about decision-making: Jeff Bezos classifies decisions into 'two-way door' and 'one-way door' types.[13] A two-way door decision is one which you can undo: If you made a wrong choice, you can always recover without too much of a financial or reputational loss. The tricky ones are the one-way door decisions, which are either impossible or too costly to reverse. The two-way door decisions are not that costly, and hence must be made quickly, and at lower levels in the organization, whereas one-way door decisions are critical, and must be made with adequate deliberation and at higher levels. Which leaves you with a very few, about 10 per cent, decisions that demand slow and deliberate thinking, involving the upper echelons of the organization. By pushing decision-making down, for 90 per cent of the cases, you retain nimbleness and people learn accountability.

I have personally found mental models very useful. For instance, when I was starting my career as an independent consultant and corporate coach, I had all sorts of individuals and companies reaching out for advice or trainings. It ranged from budding entrepreneurs seeking some confidence and advice, to large corporates wanting their leaders to be trained on design thinking or strategy. Saying 'yes' was natural, but saying 'no' was vital. And saying 'no' for a reason which is grounded in some fundamentals. So, here is the mental model that has served me well.

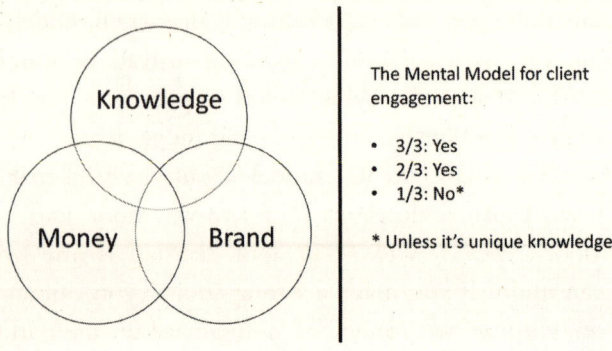

Figure 17: Mental model for going ahead with an engagement.

As with most other useful things in life, it's a simple Venn diagram. Figure 17 depicts the model comprising three parameters that determine whether I say a 'yes' or a 'no' to an incoming opportunity. The parameters are: 1) the knowledge that the client or the project offers me; 2) the brand of the client or the individual that I am engaging with; and 3) the money I am making in that engagement. The rule is that if I get a high score on any two of the three, I will say 'yes'. But if I get only one of these, then I will say a clear 'no'. However, if it were only one, then it must be 'knowledge'. Let me take a few cases to explain.

For clarity's sake, these are knowledge, brand and money associated with what the client has to offer me, and not the reverse. I would say a ready 'yes' to working with ISRO or AIIMS for the sheer learning experience, or doing programmes for a cause which I can relate to, without seeking any monetary reward. If I must consult a budding entrepreneur, I will look at enhancing my knowledge significantly, especially if the person is in genuine need of me. But it has to be earned.

However, if I am getting good enough money by doing repetitive, low value add workshops or consulting projects with yet another corporate, I would rather read a few more books or write one. If I am getting a giant brand but they aren't willing to pay me much, then it means that they don't value my knowledge or contribution and that I must cut my losses right away in such an engagement. And as you can see here, the model is virtuous. I get knowledge and brand to begin with, and then I can make money later. But the reverse isn't necessarily true. If somebody gives me money, then there is no guarantee that I will be able to later work with clients who add to my knowledge base or who are brands unto themselves.

Have I lost clients while following this mental model? Absolutely. Quite a few. But I haven't lost trust in the model. There aren't many regrets along the way, professionally. But again, I must be honest that there are days when I must work for money. For instance, when I wrote my first book, which was followed by the pandemic, I still ran a household, and for that I needed money and that's where I would go ahead with high money, low knowledge/brand kind of engagements. But the money better be serious, so that I don't abuse my mental model very often. By and large, my mental model has served me well in all contexts. It leaves me with a lot of free time—time which I can then channel at my own will. And that's real luxury.

I will urge you to think through your choices in life and construct a mental model for yourself. A rather simple rule of thumb that serves you well while you are taking important professional decisions. Especially for the one-way door kind of decisions. And these needn't even be models. They can well be statements. For instance, when working with start-up founders, especially in the early stage, I have this ironclad rule: always ask for your consulting fee. Most early stage entrepreneurs will be eager to trade their equity for my consulting hours rather than to cough up some money. But equity is cheap at this stage. And discipline is not.

Let's understand this better. Why should I ask for a consulting fee from an entrepreneur when she is rather ready to part with some of her equity for my consulting services? A couple of reasons. Firstly, a debt, or a consulting fee, disciplines both of us. For as long as I get paid, I know that my services are valued and the moment it's over I know that it's over. However, in the case of equity, it hurts nobody. I can keep dishing out irrelevant advice and I won't even know if any of it is making sense. When the entrepreneur puts hard money on the table, every minute counts.

Secondly, there's a skin in the game for both of us. If the entrepreneur is not willing to 'invest' in my advisory, then I am not sure of her commitment to her own business. I have a skin in the game, for I am as good as my last advice, and she is also tuned to get the most from the engagement. Lastly, even if she parts with 5 per cent of her equity, a 5 per cent of zero is still zero. And with more than 95 per cent of start-ups failing, I am better off cornering my cash early than staring at a pipe dream. This might sound very counter-intuitive. But it works for *me*. You need to figure out what works for you and construct your own latticework of mental models.

The approach to building mental models is three-step. Firstly, pick a domain where you need mental models urgently. These could be your hiring practices, business acquisition, partnering, investment or even career moves.

Secondly, write down the last few go/no-go decisions you made and the rough logic you adopted. Writing is the best way of thinking clearly. Finally, try putting these parameters in a parsimonious model. The simpler the better, for only the simple stuff sticks.

If you read the book carefully, you will realize that it is replete with mental models. Right from how to go about picking your fights in life to how to pitch an idea, there is a method to everything. The hope is that you will remember a few of these and then build a lot more. But you can't have it all.

Be willing to make trade-offs

The cornerstone of strategy is trade-offs—the realization that you can't have it all. You must let go of something consciously, to aim for anything of significance. Leadership, reminds Satya Nadella, means 'making choices and then rallying the team around those choices'.[14] Often these choices are hard and irreversible, as they accompany huge investments. As Nadella took over Microsoft's Server and Tools Business (STB), one of the existential questions was whether Microsoft should invest in the cloud or fight for its licence revenue for the on-premise server business (which was a cash cow).

'This might be your last job at Microsoft, because if you fail there is no parachute,' warned Steve Ballmer as he handed Nadella the top role at STB. Nadella had to make a tough decision, fast. What made the decision easy was Amazon's lead with AWS, and that Microsoft must literally refresh the way it's been used to doing business. Nadella helped the STB business adopt cloud and become relevant once again.

By February 2014, he replaced Ballmer as Microsoft's third CEO. That's how strategists live and die on trade-offs.

Trade-offs are not just limited to strategists and leaders, but also to anyone wanting to leave a trail. As Taleb reminds us, 'What matters isn't what a person has or doesn't have, it is what he or she is afraid of losing.' And that's the reason why, 'Society likes saints and moral heroes to be celibate so they do not have family pressures that may force them into the dilemma of needing to compromise their sense of ethics to feed their children.'[15] But most of us must learn to make trade-offs. And without regret.

As much as possible, it's important to be clear about what you are willing to let go. This clarity lowers your regret, for you regret greatly the opportunities foregone rather than the chances taken. Jeff Bezos' 'regret minimization framework' is in order here. At important junctures of life or business, Bezos would pose himself one question: 'At the end of my life, will I regret not having done this?' and if the answer is a 'yes' or even 'maybe', he would take the plunge.[16] That mindset gave us the world's largest online retailer and cloud operator, apart from innovations in AI and space age, among others.

You often hear senior executives who when asked to leave complain: 'I did so much for this organization. I sacrificed my personal life, missed important events to grow this company and this is what I am getting in return!' They are basically lying to themselves. The fact of the matter is that every time life posed them a choice—family or work—they chose work for the proverbial promotion. Promotion they got. Then why cry now? You got what you worked for.

Be clear about what you are willing to let go, make choices with the best of your abilities, revise them in the light of new information and experiences and, please, don't complain.

Some of the trade-offs that your profession poses are summarized in Table 1.

Span of control vs specialization: If you seek that a lot of people report to you and that you run your own bloated fiefdom, don't expect to accrue specialization. You can only be as specialist as the average of the people reporting to you, if not less, or else you can't 'manage' them well. By the way, most hierarchies are convenient ways of managing population (it's more of *where* you are than *who* you are).

Scale vs complexity: A direct postulate of the earlier dichotomy is that you can either scale your operations or enjoy doing niche, complex work. The story of the Indian IT industry is that of choosing scale over complexity—mass manufacturing over craftmanship. Both are valuable; the choice is yours. By the way, you can't make the reverse choice in this case (mass manufacturing to craftmanship).

Rapid growth vs personal time: If you must grow faster than others, you must slog harder than others (I don't quite understand smart work). McKinsey picks 'insecure overachievers', telling them in as many words that forget your family, health and personal life for the next few years, and you will jump decades. People make that choice at twenty-two, and then by thirty-five develop a slight pain on the left side of their chest!

Contacts vs content: Often, it is said, 'who you know' is more important than 'what you know'. If you know a lot of people you can escape building your content, for you will have neither the time nor the drive. But with lowering search cost and market friction, your content matters more than your contacts. Your loved ones will avoid you and interested ones will sniff you out, all owing to the gravitas of your content.

Attention to detail vs big picture view: You can't look ahead and be very mindful of your every step at the same time. You must be willing to trip along an arduous journey. The ability to think the big picture necessitates that you leave the details to others, else it's too much of a cognitive load. Be mindful that most firms don't go bust for a lack of operational efficiency but because of a want of directional clarity.

Expertise vs empathy: Expertise comes with encountering complex versions of a task over repeated accounts and then you develop predictability. You know the answer even before the question is fully stated. You choose to cut the chase by honing your judgement. You not only know but, worse still, you *think* you know it all. Well, empathy is the exact opposite. It requires deferring judgement, listening more intently, and be willing to be wrong.

Popularity vs freedom: Einstein could do what he did in the miracle year of 1905 because he was working as a patent clerk at an obscure location in Bern, and not teaching Theoretical Physics at a university in Berlin. Feynman almost declined the Nobel Prize in Physics for his fear of losing touch with reality and, more importantly, with himself. And they both declared, 'popularity is a whore'. Remember, anonymity breeds creativity.

And, of course, I haven't yet spoken about personality vs process, equity vs debt, automation vs human and, my favourite, permission vs apology. That's for you to fill up.

High span of control	Greater specialization
Scale	Complexity
Rapid growth	Time for self and family
Contacts	Content
Attention to detail	Big picture view
Expertise	Empathy
Popularity	Freedom

Table 1: Critical trade-offs in a career.

At a personal level, you make trade-offs daily. A vital one is: Should I consume today or save for tomorrow? In fact, as it turns out, spending money wisely is a greater art than earning money wisely. You can get lucky to earn some quick bucks, but not so much if you don't know how to make the money work for you. It's your spending choices that largely define your life and happiness; after all, your money is sitting as some digits in the cloud!

We often tend to spend our money in a counter-intuitive, rather a counterproductive manner. If you were to spend money on stuff that you use daily versus what you use rarely, what would you rather do? I guess, you will spend more money on frequently used stuff than the less frequently used ones. But that's precisely where our logic fails us. We tend to often spend a vulgar amount on fancy vacations, heavy jewellery, expensive dresses and other possessions which are rarely used, if ever, while cutting corners on a daily basis.

Let's look at this graph in Figure 18. The x-axis represents the Frequency of Usage—from daily to rarely; while the y-axis depicts the Expenditure, from low to high.

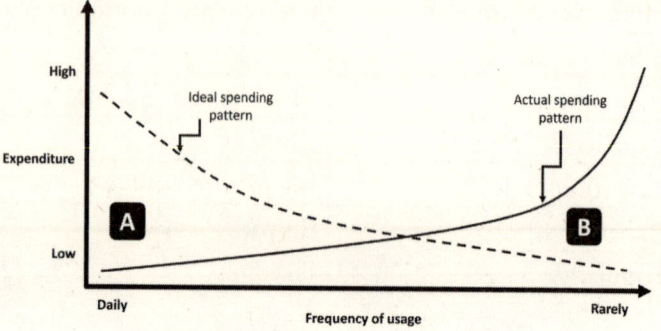

Figure 18: How to spend widely, on what matters daily.

There are two categories of expenditure:

Category A: Daily use items for consumption, such as mattress, chair/table, daily wear, food, spectacles, kitchen/ living, personal hygiene, fitness, laptop/mobile, workspace, furnishing, hobbies, books/stationery, car (interiors), entertainment and paid content, among others. The list is actually not so big, if you get to it.

Category B: Rarely used items, but very costly, such as jewellery, holidays, farmhouse, party wear, car (exteriors) and weddings. They are meant for signalling, primarily. Most people take high interest rate loans to meet their B-category desires, at the cost of A-category needs.

The simple idea I am proposing is that the stuff of regular use, which is more for consumption, should get precedence over stuff of rare usage, which is meant for signalling. I would rather spend lavishly on a chair on which I sit for seven hours daily than on a farmhouse that I visit two days in a year. But nobody sees my chair!

Basically, your expense trajectory may well be flawed. You tend to spend a lot more, proportionately, on stuff that's for others, at the cost of what's for you. You will take out that china cutlery set for a guest but will settle for steel on a daily basis. You will gift a Waterman fountain pen but will settle for a ten-bucks ballpoint for yourself, because it serves the need. You will compromise with your canteen food, which isn't terribly nutritious, on a daily basis, but go big on the Friday night parties as a host. That's what I am talking about: spending where it's visible, versus where it matters.

If the idea is to gather happiness, understand one thing: Happiness is not the intensity but the frequency of events. What will make you happier: One large increment per year, or several smaller ones over the year? Incidentally, the latter. But your employer keeps you on the hook with the once-in-a-year bonus. *The joy of life is not at the end of the turn, but along the way*. It's about the number of times you can create instances of happiness, even in small matters, than waiting for that big pay-off. Daily you have several opportunities for creating that happiness, provided you are willing to rethink your spending decisions—both of time and money.

So much for trade-offs, let's now look at how to communicate your intent well, or else you are doomed to remain frustrated.

Be politically savvy. It pays.

Has it ever happened to you that nobody seems to be interested in your genius idea? What you thought is world-changing is falling on deaf ears? Well, if you haven't experienced it yet, wait till you do. But most likely, if your memory and ego serve you well, you have certainly come across such instances where you felt like, 'what's wrong with others'. There is nothing wrong with others. It's just that you are expecting too much from your idea and yourself, without giving any proof to anybody on either's worth.

I have come across scores of talented and well-intentioned employees oozing with ideas, but with zero organizational skills. They fail to put their ideas across in a manner that makes sense to others, rally a coalition around their ideas, and build a business case. And if you think that it's not your job, think again. In the borderless world of rapid collaboration and artificial intelligence, there's hardly any prize for conjuring up wild ideas. Marks only for getting ideas through the organizational and social maze. Or else you are a sitting genius. A sitting-in-the-corner genius (sounds familiar?).

After having engaged with over 170 firms, across public and private set-ups and pan industries and nationalities, I have this conjecture to offer: *It's not the best idea that wins, but the most 'acceptable' one that does.* Acceptable to those around you: the stakeholders. I am just invoking the mechanisms of evolutionary ecology to the organizational context. The punishing vagaries of variation-selection-retention work all too well in the corporate milieu, though most tend to disagree, or don't see it in as clear terms. An idea must be selected by the environment for it to be replicated and scaled. Or else, it has no chance. And whose job is it to make that idea work? Yours, of course.

Let's take a crude analogy. Suppose you have a neighbour whom you know for the last ten years, and you are quite good friends. Does your neighbour share the same love and adoration for your five-year-old as you do? Even 5 per cent of it? Unlikely. How about your best friend? Then how can you expect some stranger in the politically sensitive office environment to love your idea which, frankly, exists only in your head? If people don't share your passion about something which is genuinely lovely (your five-year-old), how can they share a common emotion on something invisible, risky? So, it's not their fault. It's nature.

How do you make sure that your idea survives, and better still, evolves over the process? You start by identifying your key stakeholders and mapping their fears and motivations pertaining to that idea. Bear in mind that change is never easy, for all involved; for change is a political process. In fact, I will venture to state that *innovation is a political process*. And you can't afford to be politically naïve.

So, let's look at the stakeholder map. A stakeholder is anyone who is either related to the problem or the solution that you are working on. You need to firstly identify the key stakeholders. You can't afford to miss out on a stakeholder who is dormant right now but could be crucial later. Such a stakeholder can jeopardize your best laid plans. You then identify the prime fears and motivators related to the proposed idea or the plan. Since every change brings with it hope and anxiety, it's good to map these.

You may have two realizations upon this mapping. Firstly, some stakeholders may have more fears and anxieties than positives to do with your idea, as they may lose their position of power, or other valuables. Secondly, somebody's positive may become someone else's negative, as they may have conflicting interests. Automation will certainly please the production manager but not so much the head of the labour union, or that outsourcing may make the CFO look good but people in the IT team may not like it one bit. What do you do under such circumstances?

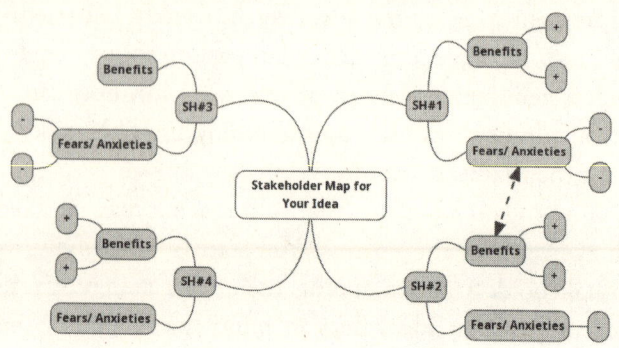

Figure 19: Stakeholder map for your idea.

As is evident from Figure 19, there are stakeholders who have more benefits than fears (Stakeholder #4), some with more anxieties than advantages (Stakeholder #3), and yet others who have a balanced take on your idea (Stakeholder #1). Also, one stakeholder's fears may be somebody else's advantage, as in the case of SH #1 and SH #2. This kind of a map, if done in advance, helps you anticipate the effect of your proposed idea and work towards a win-win situation.

In the case of a conflict between stakeholders, you have three options: 1) neutralize the stakeholder, 2) work on addressing the negatives or detractors, and 3) add positives or motivators. What will be your choice? Certainly, neutralizing won't be a pretty option, for you can't afford to alienate somebody in a multi-interaction game, because you will soon be on the receiving end. You can't address negatives beyond a point, for it may severely compromise your idea, as job displacement is a harsh reality of automation. But you can certainly be creative in coming up with some positives that will more than offset the losses and tip the balance in your favour. Job relocation, voluntary retirement, trainings for skill augmentation, etc., are viable positives in such circumstances. But don't leave these ideas to a later date. That's what being politically astute means. You anticipate the fallout of your ideas and work proactively with your various constituencies for a smooth transition, from as-is to to-be.

While creativity calls for the crazy types—the square pegs in the round hole—it also demands the capabilities to navigate the organizational milieu while marshalling such ideas to their logical conclusions. Most mavericks are just that: mavericks. If they fail to rally people around their dreams, such dreams remain private fantasies.

Bezos, a maverick himself, is quick to call out the significance of political skills in rallying any worthy idea. He maintains that a person with an idea must be able to create the conditions in which the idea flourishes. There is hardly any room for creative geniuses with zero organizational skills.[17] Because your ideas can take you only so far. One option is to partner with others who can complement you, but there again you need non-technical skills to establish that win-win equation.

To understand such skills from close quarters, let's look at the world's largest and most audacious government ID project, the Unique Identification Authority of India's (UIDAI) Aadhaar. The person in charge was Nandan Nilekani, a 1978 graduate of IIT Bombay, co-founder of Infosys, and the chairman of the UIDAI project. In July 2009, Nilekani was appointed as the chairman of the UIDAI project, in the second term of Manmohan Singh's government. Was everything and everyone in his favour?

Hardly. For starters, the Supreme Court of India gave an interim ruling that Aadhaar was voluntary and could not be mandated by any government agency for providing citizen services. The then Union Home Minister and later Finance Minister, P. Chidambaram, didn't think that the enrolment process was foolproof. The Opposition of the NDA government had its own misgivings.

The former CEO of Infosys, who was used to a big staff and many powers, was reduced to a small office in Delhi, on a shoestring budget, with less than desirable staff, all wrapped in red tape, and asked to bring to force the most audacious project till date: giving a unique identity to every Indian. As Nilekani concedes, 'I've now learnt how to deal with a lot of serious opposition, including sneak attacks from the activists, media, and some agencies. My job [at Infosys] was much more genteel, but these are no-holds-barred environments.'[18]

Do you think the engineer in Nilekani, or his personal genius, would have pulled the impossible on its own? He had to demonstrate political deftness on a project and at a scale that saw a regime change, bouts of political conflicts, ideological clashes and execution hurdles, notwithstanding the concerns around privacy and access. He built a team from scratch, starring the two IAS officers, Ram Sewak Sharma and M.S. Srikar, and Ganga K., a liberal arts major and a technology buff. The core team understood technology but, more importantly, bureaucracy, and together the 280-strong team navigated the maze at New Delhi and elsewhere.[19]

Nilekani worked tirelessly in building coalitions around ministers, bureaucrats, telecom service providers, device manufacturers, private players, Reserve Bank of India, central and private banks, and several others in expansive India. The first 100 million registrations happened by November 2011, 200 million by February 2012, and 600 million by 2014. As a testimony to Nilekani's astute nature, Srikanth Nadhamuni, former head of technology at the UIDAI, opines, 'Nandan is patient with various opinions and groups. In meetings, you'd have bureaucrats from various cadres in addition to lots of people from the corporate sector. Yet, he would take along everyone till the entire group rose to a certain level of efficiency.'[20]

Today, Aadhaar and India's digital stack is a standard bearer of public goods. From direct benefit transfer (DBT), broadening and tightening the tax net, and know your customer (KYC) authentication to vaccine registration and certification during COVID-19, Aadhaar has been the lifeline for millions of Indians.

The best laid ideas need the currency of political will and political skill, and that's no subject at a B-School. Life teaches you that, often the hard way. But it pays.

Maintain knowledge differential, not information differential

There are two ways of thriving in a competitive set-up: information differential and knowledge differential. While information differential is on the continuum of 'know what', the knowledge differential comes from 'know how', and more importantly, 'know why'.

The information asymmetry is the old way where you gain either prior or proprietary information and you withhold it to gain some mileage. Take for instance the stock market, or the uglier forms like insider trading. Hoarding information is all too pervasive in office set-ups and even across organizations, while dealing with suppliers, customers, investors, regulators or other externalities. Insecure bosses thrive on such information differentials, not realizing that they are hampering their personal progress, all the while eroding the system.

Then you have the knowledge differential, where you have both a know how and a know why, that most others don't. Since you have earned it the hard way, it's not easily tradeable. Think of long-term investing where all available information is in the public domain and yet you beat the market and other players, or the elegant game of chess where all pieces and moves are in full view and yet masters can think a couple of moves ahead.

Most serious professions inherently necessitate bridging the knowledge differential, and it happens through formal or informal teaching, mentoring, coaching or managing. Every time you are correcting your juniors' mistakes and teaching a better approach, you are diminishing your knowledge differentiation with that person. When I teach at an institute or do an executive programme, I am essentially and willingly bridging the knowledge gap—both formally and informally.

The pertinent question then is: How do you maintain the knowledge differential? Two ways: teach less, or learn more. Teaching less isn't a viable option, for if not you then somebody else will teach and you won't even know when you have become inconsequential. That leaves you with only one choice: learn more. Go not just deep into your domain but also across domains so that you build your robust body of knowledge with wider relevance. You need to develop intelligence, which is emerging from constant learning and never concluding, for as Bruce Lee reminded us: 'Styles and patterns have come to conclusion, therefore they [have] ceased to be intelligent.'[21]

A genuine knowledge differential can emerge only from within, and not without. If you seek data or information from elsewhere, everyone else also has that access, or maybe even more. What truly differentiates you is your unique ability to synthesize that information into proprietary patterns, or mental models. That's the idiosyncratic part, the difficult to copy piece. Even teachers can be of little assistance here. It's a solo journey. Conceded Khalil Gibran, 'No man can reveal to you aught but that which already lies half asleep in the dawning of your knowledge.'[22] So, delve deep within.

As Warren Buffet will assure youngsters, you are more likely to win a race that you have self-selected. Your passion is what drives you when the going gets tough and most others fall by. You are most likely to maintain a differential on your specific knowledge. Since what you are pursuing is triggered by your curiosity, and fuelled by your passion and inherent talent, you are more likely to go a lot further than somebody who is merely following the loudest and the latest. Happiness, then, will be the side effect of pursuing with full dedication a cause larger than yourself. Or as Phil Knight would put it: 'The cowards never started and the weak died along the way. That leaves us, ladies and gentlemen. Us.'[23]

A way of maintaining the knowledge differential is by being very conscious about your company.

There is an old saying: Show me your friends and I will show you your future. In today's world, you have more choice than ever to select your company. You have no reason to limit your circle to those at office, or in your society or even city or country. You can create your own microculture. But the key is to be very wise and selective with such people; they can propel you to great heights or push you into oblivion, without much of your own efforts.

When asked about how Federer pushed his game, the young Nadal is quick to establish, 'I always considered Roger like my greatest rival. So, when I arrive on tour, Roger was the guy that I had to follow. I think Roger helped me a lot to grow in all levels and that's why probably because of this rivalry at this stage of my career, in a personal way with all the injuries that I had, I always had the motivation to keep going because you're having somebody like him.'[24] That's how great champions operate. They efficiently surround themselves with greatness. At Wimbledon, the top-seeded players share locker rooms, practise together, eat together, before they compete on the field. That speaks volumes about their character.

You are defined by the kind of company you keep, especially with those who are unlike you. Both self-development and creativity come from deliberate aberration; you need to be comfortable with people who make you feel uncomfortable. You must deliberately seek divergent perspectives. Bezos is a big proponent of diversity in his leadership team and the organization, and not the diversity of the usual kind: gender, ethnicity, tenure or nationality. He actively seeks mavericks, those with a pioneering spirit, those who are sometimes annoying, of a rebellious kind.[25] Such diversity is critical, especially when you are inventing and pioneering in the absence of a customer. The different world views, experiences and dispositions in your team make up for that external voice and feedback, and you push inventions forward.

Diversity brings with it conflict, because now not everyone thinks like you. Are all conflicts unproductive? No. Organizational researcher Karen Jehn classifies workplace conflicts into two categories: relationship conflicts and task conflicts. The former are personality and emotional clashes, whereas the latter are around ideas and opinions. A longitudinal study of work groups involved in non-routine, or creative activities suggests that while task conflict enhances performance, relationship conflict hinders it.[26] In a way, it's good to have people challenging your ideas and world view without drawing animosity with your personality. They help you grow as an individual, without hurting your self-confidence, provided you are willing to have them in your life. You cultivate an environment which is tense but secure, where your creative muscles are flexed, and where you don't fear losing the person while being in an argument.

Wharton's Adam Grant advocates for building a 'challenge network' in your life. The art is to have enough common ground that you agree on a wide range of topics, and then a few disagreements are welcome so that all benefit in the process. If you are outright hostile, there is no learning and hence mutual progress. '(For) if we can't learn to find occasional glee in discovering we were wrong, it will be awfully hard to get anything right,' notes Grant.[27] And admitting being wrong is an act of courage.

You may tend to think that at least gender-based diversity is sorted in most modern corporates, but my experience indicates that it isn't. The higher you go, the fewer women you see, even in sectors like banking, hospitality, healthcare and IT services. That beats my understanding. Anatomically speaking, women tend to use both hemispheres when speaking and processing verbal information, whereas men tend to use one. Men tend to think in gist, whereas women typically remember the details. Women pay a lot more attention to non-verbal cues, men don't. Women tend to be more adept at empathizing, men at executing. And that's where a diverse group makes sense for creative performance. Including more women in your workforce can show immediate mileage on creativity and productivity.

How often have you told yourself and others that, 'I tried hard, but . . .' Life is much like Maths: little grace for right steps or intent, full marks for the correct answer. While previously I have glorified the importance of planning as a skill, stating that plans may fail but planning doesn't, here's the real deal: You can't afford to slavishly follow a 'great' plan. A plan is only as good as its relevance to the current reality and, hence, you must learn to work on your plan as you are executing it. The deal is to own the outcome, and not the plan.

Robin Sharma maintains that real change happens through personal mastery and self-responsibility.[28] You must take charge of the piece of the puzzle called your life. There will always be several uncontrollable factors but, still, you have to own up to some of the central pieces. It all starts by owning your thoughts, your actions and their outcome. If you are willing to think through a situation, and to accept the outcome without questioning 'Why me?', you don't have anything to fear. The problem happens when you take an action to escape self-examination, and then look for excuses, or vulnerable others, when things hit an impasse.

The following lines by Edwin Markham are instructive here:[29]

For all your days prepare,
And meet them ever alike:
When you are the anvil, bear—
When you are the hammer, strike.

Hope you continue investing in maintaining a knowledge differential, with humility.

6

Leadership Is a Choice Not Everyone Can Make

'When it comes to standards, as a leader, it's not what you preach, it's what you tolerate.'

—Jocko Willink[1]

On the sunny morning of 10 August 1979, a team of scientists and engineers had gathered at Sriharikota, a barrier island off the Bay of Bengal coast. The occasion was the launch of India's Satellite Launch Vehicle (SLV-3), designed and developed indigenously by a tireless team with a shoestring budget at ISRO. An all solid, four-stage vehicle weighing seventeen tonnes and with a height of twenty-three metres, SLV-3 was India's experimental flight intended to place the forty-kilo Rohini satellite into the Low Earth Orbit. Just 317 seconds into the flight, owing to fuel leakage, the rocket burst into flames and the satellite was lost to the Bay of Bengal.

The project leader was a forty-eight-year-old engineer from Rameswaram. It was his first large-scale failure, and it went quite public. The question was: Who would face the wrath of the media after having 'thrown' crores of taxpayers' money into the Bay of Bengal? So, the then chairman of ISRO, Satish Dhawan, stepped up and took on the media, famously declaring, 'We failed! But I have very strong trust in my team, and I believe that next time we will definitely succeed.'

On 18 July 1980, the launch was successful, making India only the sixth member of an exclusive club of nations who had begun conquering space. And this time, Dhawan asked Kalam to address the press conference. Years later, Kalam, the Missile-Man of India, would fondly recall the first principle of leadership: 'When the failure occurred, the leader owned it up. When the success came, he gave the credit to his team.'[2] That's the ISRO culture for you and how they produce leaders.

Today, ISRO stands tall in the space of space exploration, much to the pride of Indians and the envy of our regional neighbours. The institution has built a pipeline of leaders, those who have personally and publicly taken risk, faced the flak and remained true to their purpose. They are not mere managers, they espouse commitment, confidence and courage. In the words of Jim Collins, they 'blend extreme personal humility with intense professional will.'[3] They are the Level-5 leaders.

Let's understand how they do it.

You can't manage enough to suddenly start leading

As the saying goes: *You can't pile together enough good people to make a great one.* Similarly, you can't be a manager enough to now become a leader. Most people think that leading is a superlative form of managing—if you manage a large enough team and manage people who manage such teams, ergo, you are a leader. No. You are just a manager, or a general manager at best, but not a leader. A leader is not necessarily a manager, neither a manager a leader, notwithstanding the title.

So, if you think you will eventually become a leader after having cut your teeth managing scores of people, be assured that it takes more than your bloated reporting structure for that leap to happen. No doubt, your experience in managing teams offers you credibility, but to take your team to a place where they have never been takes more than a few techniques. You need imagination. It takes you to envisage a future that they haven't seen yet, and a path towards it, and the courage to walk the path, often against the establishment. Notes Shantanu Narayen, the India-born CEO of Adobe, 'Every leader must be a flag planter and a road builder—setting an inspiring vision and clearing a path for teams to take ownership and execute.'[4] The rest all are managers.

According to former US President Bill Clinton, the four components of leadership are: *envisioning* the future, *explaining* the current situation and the approach forward, *including* the various stakeholders and *executing* your objectives.[5] Out of envision, explain, include and execute, I guess, the differentiating feature is envision, and most managers struggle there. Ergo, they are good at maintaining the status quo and not attempting a paradigm shift.

The defining distinction between a manager and a leader is that the former works on increasing the efficiency and even effectiveness within the same orbit, whereas the latter aims at an orbital shift. Managers are busy maintaining operational efficiencies, whereas leaders are busy planting new experiments. Once a few experiments show results and it's time to standardize the new, managers come to the party. In short, managers maintain orbits that leaders create.

The orbit shifting necessitates generating the escape velocity and stability in the new orbit. You can't launch a satellite and hope that it reaches somewhere. You must go from certainty to certainty with wild explorations in between.

How do you propel an orbit shift? ISRO has shown us the way.

It was in 1962 that a band of young engineers and scientists, on loan from institutes like Department of Atomic Energy (DAE) in Bombay, Aeronautical Development Establishment (ADE) in Bangalore, and Physical Research Laboratory (PRL) in Ahmedabad, among others, were sent on a rocketry training trip to NASA's Goddard Space Flight Center at Beltsville, Maryland. Their boss was a Cambridge-educated scion of a wealthy business family from Gujarat: Vikram Sarabhai. A charming physicist and an astronomer who was trained under none other than Sir Chandrasekhara Venkata Raman, Sarabhai could get the best of engineers from government-backed establishments to work for his dream: to establish India's very own space research organization against the backdrop of a country still gaining its feet and battling poverty, illiteracy and vestiges of colonialism. He charmed Indian scientists studying in the US and the UK to join his experiments with sounding rockets in the coastal town of Thumba, near Thiruvananthapuram, Kerala. He was setting us up for the space age, on a shoestring budget, all because of his vision, resourcefulness and boldness.

When questioned on why India must spend so much on such an uncertain trajectory, Sarabhai famously retorted:[6]

> There are some who question the relevance of space activity in a developing nation. To us, there is no ambiguity of purpose. We do not have the fantasy of competing with economically advanced nations in the explorations of the moon and the planets or manned space flight. But we are convinced that if we are to play a meaningful role nationally, and in the comity of nations, we must be second to none in the application of advanced technologies to the real problems of man and society, which we find in our own country.
>
> One of the most important benefits of space research lies in the spin-off which follows. I might illustrate this from the experience which we are gaining in the development of rockets. This involves new disciplines and an understanding of materials and methods; of close tolerances and testing under extremes; the development of guidance and control and the use of advanced information techniques. When one succeeds, it is through the working together of a large number of specialists who dedicate themselves to a common task. Indeed, I often feel that the discipline and the culture of the new world which emerges through the pursuit of activities of this type are among the most important from the standpoint of a developing nation.

He had no ambiguity of purpose. So, here we are today, discovering water on the lunar surface, searching for signs of life on Mars, preparing for a manned mission to the Moon, and all of this with a world-beating frugality.

As a side note: In 1962, Indians had some company at NASA. We had engineers from West and East Pakistan also getting trained in rocketry. In fact, Pakistan had a head start in space research, as they had formed their Space & Upper Atmosphere Research Commission (SUPARCO) in September 1961. Whereas, Indian National Committee for Space Research (INCOSPAR), the predecessor of ISRO, was formally established only in 1962. But the paths forked out, not owing to a staggered start or funding, but leadership. As R. Aravamudan, one of the engineers from the historic 1962 batch to NASA, attests, 'Without Sarabhai India's space programme might have ended in the same doldrums as Pakistan's.'[7]

That's what leadership can do. And that's a choice not everyone can make.

If you study leadership, the cornerstone is how one reacts to failure.

The SLV-3 failure fortified Kalam's resolve and established the leadership of Satish Dhawan as the one who could take on criticism from the highest levels. Of the four ASLV (Augmented Satellite Launch Vehicle) launched between 1987 and 1994, three failed. In fact, the very first PSLV (Polar Satellite Launch Vehicle) launched on 20 September 1993 failed. But, after a series of modifications and improvements, PSLV emerged as India's workhorse and one of the world's most reliable launchers in that payload category. With a success rate of 94 per cent, as of 22 May 2023, the PSLV has made fifty-seven launches, sending over 300 satellites for more than thirty countries.[8]

If you read carefully about these launches in the ISRO archive, you will come across an interesting regularity.

Most of the mission directors who led a failed or a partially successful test launch emerged to become ISRO's chairman or a site head.[9] Madhavan Nair was the mission director of the maiden PSLV launch in 1993. Nair went on to become ISRO's chairman between 2003 and 2009. K. Sivan was the director for GSLV-D5 which was fuelled by indigenously built cryogenic engines and was launched in January 2014, and he led ISRO from 2018 to 2022. P. Kunhikrishnan, who was the director for a record thirteen missions, headed the U.R. Rao Satellite Centre in Bangalore between 2018 and 2021. Of course, Kalam, who was the mission director of the very first SLV-3, which failed, went on to become India's President.

The same pattern is seen elsewhere, too.

Some of the most celebrated and transformative leaders emerged when they were thrown into unprecedented challenges. They took on high stakes projects, delivered and then were betted upon again. Sundar Pichai, the current chief of Alphabet, started his career working on the Google Toolbar that would enable Microsoft Internet Explorer and Mozilla Firefox users to conveniently access Google's search engine. He then took on the highly ambitious Chrome project, which pitted Google directly against Microsoft. His efforts led to Google securing over 50 per cent market share in web browsers and in succeeding Larry Page as the firm's CEO.

Andy Jassy filled in the big shoes of Jeff Bezos at Amazon for his work at Amazon Web Services, which incidentally was never Amazon's core business. But it became a category by itself. Satya Nadella got the top spot at Microsoft for his successful turnaround of the company's enterprise servers and cloud computing business and giving a good fight to

Amazon through Microsoft Azure. Arvind Krishna, the IBM CEO, is credited with transforming the century-old company with the high-profile merger and integration of Red Hat and genuinely embracing the open source wave. Natarajan Chandrasekaran became the first non-Parsi to head the 150-year-old Tata Group, owing to his stellar performance at TCS, which happens to offer the highest dividends to the group. Not to forget the man from Ranchi who was asked to lead a rookie team to the inaugural T20 World Cup, and who returned home with the cup.

What does this tell you about leadership? It goes to show that unless you take risks, have a skin in the game, go through difficult experiences and soak in failure, and don't give up, you don't deserve to be a leader. Till such time, you are simply a manager. Rather, I would argue that leaders have a soul in the game, and not just skin.

Have a soul in the game, not just skin

When the fragile, Sanskrit-chanting thirty-eight-year-old theoretical physicist, Robert Oppenheimer, was asked to lead the Manhattan Project at the Los Alamos Laboratory during World War II, his first task was to recruit the best and the brightest for an important, yet uncertain mission. A full-time professor at the University of California, Berkeley, Oppenheimer hardly had any leadership, let alone military experience. And yet he is dubbed as the 'Father of the Atomic Bomb'. How did he manage to get the likes of Enrico Fermi, Albert Einstein, Richard Feynman, Neils Bohr, Ernest Lawrence and Hans Bethe, among other greats, to work under his leadership, let alone work together? He showed something bigger to the 2,000-odd engineers and scientists: The Purpose. He was in it fully, not just a skin in the game, but the very soul.

Oppenheimer wrote about his trepidations with the young recruits:[10]

> Many were put off by the military nature of the project and the notion of disappearing into the New Mexico desert for an indeterminate period. . . . But there was another side to it. Almost everyone realized that this was a great undertaking. Almost everyone knew that if it were completed successfully and rapidly enough, it might determine the outcome of the war. Almost everyone knew that it was an unparalleled opportunity to bring to bear the basic knowledge and art of science for the benefit of his country. Almost everyone knew that this job, if it were achieved, would be part of history. This sense of excitement, of devotion, and of patriotism in the end prevailed. Most of those with whom I talked came to Los Alamos.

It might appear to you as an easy sell, but it was nothing but, till Oppenheimer was in it, fully and irreversibly. That's what the followers look at: Is my commander taking the bullet?

Ever heard of General Sam Manekshaw? He was India's first field marshal, a five-star general who never retired. 'Sam Bahadur', as he was fondly called, served in the Indian Army for over fifty years: spanning World War II, Indo-Pakistani War of 1947, Sino-Indian War of 1962, Indo-Pakistani War of 1965, and Indo-Pakistani War of 1971. He was the hero of the 1971 war and was made a Field Marshal in 1973.

In 1990, during a lecture at St Xavier's College, Bombay, Gen. Manekshaw elucidated the following attributes of a leader: professional knowledge and competence, ability to take a decision and own it, justice and impartiality, moral and physical courage, loyalty towards his people, humanness, discipline and character.[11] On the debate of whether leaders are born or made, he was clear that leaders are made and that if you gave him a person with reasonable common sense and decency, he could make a leader out of the person. He emphasized a lot on the aspects of owning up to yourself, your decisions, your men and your country. His greatest achievement in his long and illustrious career was that he never punished anybody in his command.[12] At one point, he was commanding over a million men. With so much power, what he had was his soul in the game. And his men knew it.

To bring home the point, let's revisit the 1971 war, the last time India and Pakistan had a large-scale military rendezvous. For several months, persecuted East Pakistan refugees were making their way to India. India's Prime Minister, Indira Gandhi, decided that military action was in order, or else thousands of East Pakistanis would die at the hands of West Pakistan. The initial orders were for April 1971, but Gen. Manekshaw refused to engage in a war, as it would have meant a slow movement of his fleet towards Bengal, flooding of the Ganges basin, an open invitation to China to attack us and several other logistical limitations, ensuring a swift defeat. Finally, when he launched the assault on 3 December 1971, it was all over in thirteen days. In less than a fortnight, the Pakistani Army surrendered, and a nation was born: Bangladesh.

The Indian Army took over 93,000 prisoners of war as an aftermath and held them for over eighteen months. The manner in which these prisoners of war were treated by the Indian Army was remarkable and historical. They slept in barracks, while the Indian soldiers slept in open tents. They were given the best food, medical care and even the Quran. Gen. Manekshaw received a lot of flak from his leadership, including Indira Gandhi, but he retorted that these were soldiers and they had fought well and hard, and that it was his duty to take care of them.[13] There is little doubt that, he was the favourite on both sides of the border.

Putting your team ahead of your personal goals and ambitions is typical of the armed forces. When a newly commissioned officer joins a unit, he is not allowed to step into the officers' mess for the first two or three months. He must sleep with his men, cook food, clean the barracks, be a sentry for a couple of nights in a row, know each jawan's family and their issues, and only when they think he is ready is he allowed to step into the officers' mess. In fact, in some Gorkha units, an officer is expected to speak Nepali fluently before being allowed to command them. And that's why it's said that your title makes you a manager, but it's your people who make you a leader. If your jawans don't trust you and know that you could lead them in the face of adversity, nothing can save you. An officer's appraisal is often written by his men and not by his commanding officer.

To look at a different example, it was the genius and courage of Walt Disney who persisted in experimenting with *Snow White and the Seven Dwarfs* even when his brother Roy Disney and several competing studios thought that the idea of a full-length feature film was wasteful. But Walt persisted.

While securing a $500,000 loan from the Bank of America, he single-handedly enacted the script, scene by scene, to the bank's officers. Walt wrote years later, 'All these years I've been taking the bows for the cartoons and the animated features. I did that for a purpose: to establish the Disney name as a guarantee to the public of good family entertainment.'[14] He bet on his own reputation to usher in an era of animation, in colour and with sound. And then hundreds of animators and artists stood on the shoulders of Disney and his studio, offering timeless entertainment.

When you set out to create something meaningful, something larger than yourself and more enduring than your time on Earth, you need to assemble a handful of those who have a soul in the game. To put it simple, they are driven.

And this ethos is adequately clear from this admission of Phil Knight, the creator of Nike:[15]

It was us against the world, and we felt damned sorry for the world. That is, when we weren't righteously pissed off at it. Each of us has been misunderstood, misjudged, dismissed. Shunned by bosses, spurned by luck, rejected by society, short-changed by fate when looks and other natural graces were handed out. We'd each been forged by early failure. We'd each given ourselves to some quest, some attempt at validation or meaning, and fallen short.

If you get that kind of a team together, not much needs to be left to chance.

A harsh lesson Musk learned while starting Zip2 and X.com is the imperative of having full control of your business. In both the instances, he was sidelined, a crude reminder of what happened to Steve Jobs at Apple during the mid-1980s. But at SpaceX and Tesla, he didn't leave much to chance. He pumped in so much of his personal capital that he could not be ousted, and that's when he took some giant technological leaps and pushed his teams towards the limit, quite physically. 'I don't want to seem like a Johnny-come-lately or that I'm chasing a fad or just being opportunistic. I'm not an investor,' declares Musk. 'I like to make technologies real that I think are important for the future and useful in some sort of way.'[16] And you know that he is not doing all this just for money.

Who produces Christopher Nolan's movies? Nolan himself, along with his wife Emma Thomas and brother Jonathan Nolan. All the movies. And that's why he can afford to crash a real Boeing-747 plane in *Tenet*, flip over the giant truck in *The Dark Knight*, deploy the 1957-built French destroyer, Maille-Breze, for *Dunkirk*, and perform an actual large-scale explosion for *Oppenheimer*. And who can forget the larger-than-life sets during the filming of *Interstellar* and *Inception*. Nolan calls film-making a balance between technical expertise, the technical expectations of the audience and then the storytelling. There are few in the business who do cross-cutting of scenes, non-linear and layered storytelling, and keep the element of time palpable throughout the movie as he does. All this, because he writes the cheque.

Nolan is also famous for his aversion for adopting computer graphics or temp music in his movies. He insists on creating original scores along the movie that fit right on to the scene and the storyline. He makes it a point to never look at the two-dimensional monitor but instead keeps his eye fixed on the camera to experience how an audience would be viewing the actual scene. If he wants a close-up, he will take the camera all the way to an artist's face, instead of using the lenses. He wants to keep the physical relation between the audience and the actor in perspective, at all times.[17] It comes up menacingly well with Heath Ledger in *The Dark Knight*, or Cillian Murphy in *Oppenheimer*.

As a side note, who produced the *Mission Impossible* series? You would have guessed it by now: Tom Cruise. Now you understand the meaning of having your soul in the game.

Let's close this section with the Manhattan Project. Here's what Edward Teller, the father of the hydrogen bomb and the one who wasn't a big fan of Oppenheimer, says about the man's leadership style at Los Alamos. 'Oppie knew in detail what was going on in every part of the Laboratory. He was incredibly quick and perceptive in analyzing human as well as technical problems . . . He knew how to organize, cajole, humor, soothe feelings—how to lead powerfully without seeming to do so.' Notes Teller, 'He was an exemplar of dedication, a hero who never lost his humanness. Disappointing him somehow carried with it a sense of wrongdoing. Los Alamos's amazing success grew out of the brilliance, enthusiasm and charisma with which Oppenheimer led it.'[18]

Oppenheimer didn't go to a B-School for that. He just led it from his heart and guts.

Taking risk personally is one aspect, but enabling your team to play bold is quite another. And that's where leaders differ markedly from managers. Leaders fuel risk; managers contain risk.

Offer your team air cover, while they experiment wildly

Imagine that you land in a foreign country on a one-way ticket, with barely enough money for a week's survival, and not a place to stay. Your uncle, who you thought would shelter you, is long gone and you are fending off cold winters while working at a farm and lumber mill, under harsh conditions and at undignified hourly wages. Over the next three years, you write code, assemble brilliance around you, work like a dog and suddenly you become a millionaire. That is Elon Musk at age twenty-two.

And then you pump all of your money into developing reusable rockets, an idea that the mighty NASA has long foregone and is deemed a sure shot to bankruptcy. Your first mission is a public failure and so is your second and third, and you barely have enough capital to put the fourth rocket at the launch site, fearing the worst. That's not all, you are parallelly attempting to ramp up a start-up in an industry where the last successful new company was Chrysler in 1925. And all this by betting almost all of your money. That's daring, if not outright crazy.

Here's how Musk reacted to the failure of his maiden launch of Falcon-1, on 24 March 2006, at the Marshall Islands. He wrote to his team: [19]

A friend of mine wrote to remind me that only 5 of the first 9 Pegasus launches succeeded; 3 of 5 for Ariane; 9 of 20 for Atlas; 9 of 21 for Soyuz; and 9 of 18 for Proton. Having experienced firsthand how hard it is to reach orbit, I have a lot of respect for those that persevered to produce

the vehicles that are mainstays of space launch today . . .
SpaceX is in this for the long haul and, come hell or high
water, we are going to make this work.

And finally, on 28 September 2008, six years after SpaceX was
formed, the start-up had its first successful launch, delivering
a 165-kilogram non-functional boilerplate spacecraft into
low Earth orbit. That made SpaceX the first company to
register a successful orbital launch of any privately funded
and developed fully liquid-propelled carrier rocket.[20] Later,
it became the only private company to dock with the
International Space Station.

While Musk may and does come across as an alpha male,
an unreasonable capitalist, he is deeply passionate about what
he wants and is fiercely protective about his team. He pushes
them hard, often to breaking point, but he chips along, and
that's what psychological safety is about. Having your people
believe that they won't be reprimanded for failure as long as
they fail on a pursuit that is grand and worthwhile. 'They
believe that they will not be punished or humiliated for
speaking up with ideas, questions, concerns, or mistakes,' notes
Harvard's Amy Edmondson, an authority on the subject.[21]
But performance comes with a combination of psychological
safety and accountability of excellence, where people get into
their learning zone and deliver high performance.

Musk is a master of balancing psychological safety and an
accountability of excellence. Three failures, on private money,
would have deflated anybody. But Musk is no ordinary leader.
A Bachelor of Science in Physics and Economics from the
Wharton School, Musk learnt rocketry almost entirely by
reading books like *Rocket Propulsion Elements*, *Fundamentals*

of *Astrodynamics*, and *Aerothermodynamics of Gas Turbine and Rocket Propulsion*, along with several more seminal texts. No fancy engineering degree or a PhD.

Here's what Kevin Watson, an aerospace veteran for over thirty years and formerly with NASA/JPL, says about Musk:[22]

> If he asks you a question, you learn very quickly not to go give him a gut reaction. He wants answers that get down to the fundamental laws of physics. One thing he understands really well is the physics of the rockets. He understands that like nobody else. The stuff I have seen him do in his head is crazy. He can get in discussions about flying a satellite and whether we can make the right orbit and deliver Dragon at the same time and solve all these equations in real time.

That's a veteran commenting on somebody who's got there by reading books (that's why, read books!).

When leaders initiate an orbital shift, they must offer their team air cover, so that the team can experiment wildly without fearing for their careers. That's how venture capitalists usher in inventions, by underwriting the risk of ruin. A well-endowed research lab, somewhere at MIT or Caltech, can afford to explore the frontiers of science, for their failure is backed by institutions. Engineers and scientists at ISRO and NASA can shoot for the Moon, for they know that their failures in the pursuit of the new won't be tantamount to getting fired. While there might be instances of a moral hazard, if you take sufficient care of the incoming talent and build robust routines, you don't have to indulge in micromanagement or constantly fear the worst.

When in 1943, the thirty-three-year-old engineer Clarence L. 'Kelly' Johnson was asked by the US government to build its first jet fighter to take on the mighty German Luftwaffe, he signed a historic pact with his employer, Lockheed Martin. He would assemble a team of select engineers and scientists to build a top-secret department, one which was not encumbered with any bureaucracy, with minimal reporting, and that took orders only from divisional presidents or higher. He called the team *Skunk Works*.

The team of twenty-three engineers and thirty support staff managed to scavenge a place next to Lockheed's Burbank plant's wind tunnel and made quarters out of wood from discarded engine boxes. The work was kept so secretive that even janitors or secretaries were not allowed inside. The team was tasked to design a jet fighter in 180 days. In the middle of WW II, the team managed to deliver a prototype of P-80 Shooting Star in just 143 days. The team, officially known as the Lockheed Advanced Development Projects (ADP), went on to produce America's first supersonic jet F-104 Starfighter, the long-range reconnaissance plane U-2, the SR-71 Blackbird which flies at Mach-3, and the F-117A Nighthawk stealth fighter-bomber. It was only after the Soviet Union toppled that the work of Skunk Works was declassified.

Kelly Johnson listed the fourteen rules of managing innovative teams, highlighting the importance of small, autonomous teams, keeping outsiders out, and keeping reports to a minimum but documenting all critical milestones.[23]

The rules are as applicable to any team today as they were when drafted almost eighty years ago. Johnson was, above all, a leader who gave his team air cover to go bold and crazy, while personally keeping all distractions at bay.

As Warren Bennis writes in his book, *Organizing Genius*, 'At the Skunk Works, Johnson made it clear that he, not one of his subordinates, would be the person who donned suit and tie and interacted with Washington honchos . . . He did everything he could to protect his group from the meddling of corporate "suits", the bean counters and go-by-the-book types who can so easily undermine a creative enterprise by trying to tame it and bring it under corporate control.'[24]

Johnson might not have been terribly liked by his people, and neither was Steve Jobs nor is Elon Musk, but their teams respect them. They are (were) willing to take personal risks for them because they knew that their leaders would watch their backs.

At Xerox, it was the mercurial Bob Taylor who led the team of computer scientists at the PARC's Computer Science Laboratory from 1970 through 1983, and his style was such that he would literally put his body between his team and the bureaucracy at Xerox. His team of about four dozen scientists and engineers pretty much created every important technology in computers that we know of today: the graphical user interface, icons, pop-up menus, cut-and-paste techniques, overlapping windows, bitmap displays, easy-to-use word processing programmes, and Ethernet networking technologies, among others.[25]

As a leader, you must be willing to face the flak of your audience, their critiques, to ensure that your team performs. It also means that you have to be willing to sacrifice the short-term returns for long-term gains. Never easy, especially when most businesses play to the tune of markets. Bear in mind that leadership is not a popularity contest. It's about getting the extraordinary done through ordinary talent.

Here's an insightful piece of advice by Sam Walton. For context, this was written in the late 1980s and makes sense even today (maybe more so):[26]

> As business leaders, we absolutely cannot afford to get all caught up in trying to meet the goals that some retail analyst or financial institution in New York sets for us on a ten-year plan spit out of a computer that somebody set to compound at such-and-such a rate. If we do that, we take our eye off the ball. But if we demonstrate in our sales and our earnings every day, every week, every quarter, that we're doing our job in a sound way, we will get the growth we are entitled to, and the market will respect us in a way that we deserve.

This requires courage. But more importantly, clarity. And that's perhaps why leaders who aren't sure of their candidature for even the next quarter can't bet big.

You don't have to go very far to see this behaviour in action. Watch the award ceremonies of the Indian cricket team lifting the T20 WC in 2007, the ICC WC in 2011 and the Champions Trophy in 2013. Each time, the captain was M.S. Dhoni and, on each occasion, as he was awarded the cup, he didn't waste a moment handing it over to the team and disappearing to the sidelines. And now watch the post media briefing for the ICC WC 2015 when India was ousted by Australia down under and the several press conferences where Dhoni was on the receiving end of the bashing. He chose to face the wrath while at the losing end and let the team take the centre stage at a win, akin to what Kalam called the hallmark of a great leader.

You can act this way only if you are secure yourself. If you are not constantly looking for external validation, and you offer psychological safety to your team, provide them the air cover, and propel them to a higher orbit.

Design a climate through asymmetric incentives

There is an insightful saying in management: *There are two ways of being creative. One can sing and dance. Or one can create an environment in which singers and dancers flourish.*[27]

One of the mistakes most managers, and even a few annotated leaders, commit is that they attempt to change the culture of their organization in a wholesale fashion. It's like wanting India to be an innovative country before ISRO starts to think of rocket science. That's too much to ask for. Instead, let's focus on changing the *climate*. Climate, which is a local affair, is far malleable for a leader to influence than the imposing culture. Culture has inertia, and for good reasons, whereas climate always changes, and nobody feels awkward about it. That's what effective leaders are capable of. They can take a stalling, almost sinking organization, and turn it around.

'People will do something—including changing their behavior—only if it can be demonstrated that doing so is in their own best interests as defined by their own values,' notes Marshall Goldsmith.[28] Followers often need a reference point to go from here to there, while finding the journey meaningful, personally. And effective leaders act both as flag planter and road builder.

That's why leaders must model the behaviour that they expect from others. They take extreme ownership of their teams, their departments, their missions and do something so exceptional that others feel inspired, or at least embarrassed at not being a part of the change. And then, slowly, the snowball picks up momentum. But it starts with the climate. And taking ownership is never easy. 'The difficulty we have in accepting responsibility for our behavior lies in the desire to avoid the pain of the consequences of that behavior,' notes the famous psychiatrist M. Scott Peck. 'The best decision-makers are those who are willing to suffer the most over their decisions but still retain their ability to be decisive.'[29] That's what ownership looks like, for yourself and for those whom you lead.

In his Pulitzer prize-winning book, *Guns, Germs, and Steel*, the American geographer and historian Jared Diamond notes, 'History followed different course for different people because of differences among peoples' environment, not because of biological differences among peoples themselves.'[30] Bringing the discussion back to an organizational context, employee behaviours are defined more by their local environment than their innate talent or disposition. Drawn straight from the broken windows theory of criminology, your immediate environment offers you cues on appropriate behaviour. If you change people's immediate surroundings and model the appropriate behaviour, they will change—whether it's your child or your employee.

If you want your employees to be more creative, foster an office space that doesn't stink of hierarchy or even rigid order, offers sufficient free space for people to gather and ideate, provide material to prototype, organize funds to run quick and dirty experiments, expect fewer forms to be filled, and give sufficient cues that it's okay to fail occasionally, provided they are learning something new.

One of the powerful means of influencing behaviour in an organization, especially when it comes to encouraging risk-taking and innovation, is exercising asymmetric incentives. Figure 20 depicts the model of asymmetric incentives.

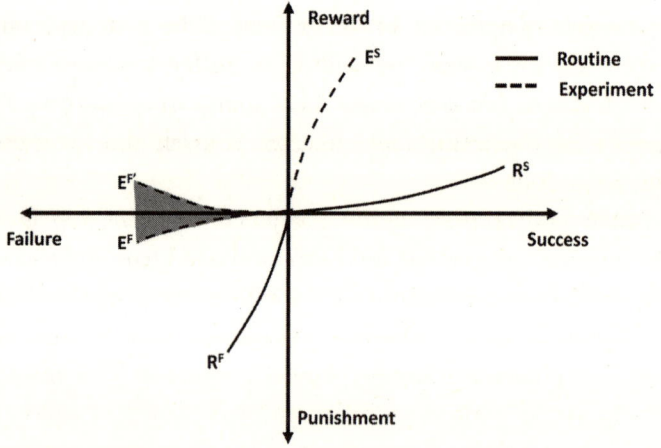

Figure 20: The power of asymmetric incentives.

Let's understand the figure better. On the x-axis, you have the outcome of an event—success or failure; and on the y-axis, you have the organizational response—reward or punishment. You can broadly have two types of activities, whether in an organizational context or in a personal realm:

routines and experiments. A routine activity is typically automatic, effortless, predictable, low-risk and forms a large chunk of one's day job. An experiment, on the other hand, is characterized by its high risk profile, is effortful, unpredictable, and comprises a very scant portion of one's job profile. Even scientists and artists would rather have over 70 per cent of their work as routine and they experiment only on the margins. Alas, there's not much of an experiment in most roles. Not that they are unamicable for experimentation. But routines are preferred, any day.

Let's understand how leaders could design an incentive system to promote systematic experimentation, ergo personal creativity and organizational innovation. If you perform a routine activity and succeed (R^S), the organization must reward you only mildly, for you are supposed to perform a routine task flawlessly. However, if you fail in performing that routine activity (R^F), the firm should reprimand you severely, as you can see a steep slope on the punishment axis. No excuse for failing in something that you are adept at.

As for experimentation, if you succeed even mildly in an experiment, the firm should reward you generously (E^S), for the leader would want to encourage a culture of risk-taking and entrepreneurship. However, upon a failed experimentation, the leader must decide between rewarding and acknowledging the attempt ($E^{F'}$) or reprimanding slightly (E^F). The choice of the response depends on the state of innovation at the organization—if risk-taking and experimentation is a rarity, then go with a mild reward on a failed innovation, and if the innovation scene is matured, you may choose to gently rap them on the knuckles if there's continued failure. After all, there must be some cost of failure, or else the motivation to succeed isn't strong.

That's your asymmetric incentives at play. The rewards and punishments are not symmetric for both routines and experiments. You shouldn't confuse a failed attempt with a wasted effort. Unless there is a genuine sense of ambiguity and uncertainty, it's all routine.

Now let's take this discussion forward and understand how machines change the equation. What do you think machines are good at: routines or experiments? I assume machines are great at performing routine tasks, without much of a fuss. And if your typical day is characterized by 90 per cent of routine tasks, aren't you inviting machines right into your back door to take over your entire career? You must incorporate systematic experiments in your life and your work. That's one surefire way of keeping machines at bay.

From an organizational context, by incentivizing experimentation, you form new routines and retire older ones, and keep your employees always a step ahead of machines. While machines can offer serious help in performing experiments, as any scientist would testify, the call on success or failure, or abandonment and perseverance, is still very much human.

Let me conclude by offering that if money can't motivate somebody and if the nature of work can't motivate that person, then even you can't. The best is for you to take another look at the nature of the work and make it inherently exciting and rewarding. You can then design the incentives around the work in such a way that calculated risk-taking becomes more appealing. You must drive your team away from enjoying the routine to indulging in experimentations. As behavioural psychologists Richard Thaler and Cass Sunstein would say, you have to be a *choice architect* for your team, for them to embrace the appropriate behaviour without them being forced (or at least perceived as being forced).[31]

Elon Musk inadvertently plays by this rule. He would brutally reprimand anybody who's not up to expectations on routine (with a little bit of stretch) tasks, but would be celebratory of failed experiments, provided there's a giant leap forward. He selects his talent very carefully, often spending hours in the end interviewing candidates, and marshalling his troops, literally, at a breakneck speed. 'He has the most talented people in the aerospace industry working for him, and the same case can be made for Tesla,' notes Peter Thiel, a pal of Musk. 'Both companies were designed with this vision of motivating a critical mass of talented people to work on inspiring things.'[32]

If you take care of your talent density, give them an audacious goal; you can then afford to step back and cut them some slack. All you need is well-engineered incentive mechanisms. They won't let you down. But don't push them too hard, or else you will lose them, permanently. And that's where being vulnerable yourself becomes vital.

Be vulnerable by choice

Sir Ken Robinson, one of the most influential educationalists and proponents of creativity in early education, narrates an interesting interaction he once had with the Dalai Lama. In an audience of over 2,000 people, Robinson was chairing a panel discussion when somebody asked the Dalai Lama a question. The spiritual guru took almost a minute in silence to gather his thoughts and finally admitted, 'I don't know.' Everyone was taken by surprise. How can His Holiness not have an answer? Just imagine the courage it takes for someone of his authority to publicly admit his ignorance. But there was the Dalai Lama, perfectly comfortable admitting his limitation. The question is not important, nor is the answer, nor the occasion. What matters is the attitude of humility. The courage of being vulnerable, by choice.

Vulnerability is the ability to give up control over a situation and trust those around you. Leaders, by their stated position and earned overconfidence, often find it difficult to let go. At some level, the inability to delegate is a manifestation of not choosing to be vulnerable, and at a larger level, you just don't trust anybody. What's surprising is that you need to start trusting others before they are obliged to earn it. As Goldsmith incisively notes, 'If you put all your cards in someone else's hands that person will treat you better than if you kept the cards to yourself.'[33] You can try this at home as well. Except we don't want to be vulnerable, for it's considered a sign of weakness.

'When experts express doubt, they become more persuasive,' notes Adam Grant. 'When someone knowledgeable admits uncertainty, it surprises people, and they end up paying more attention to the substance of the argument.'[34] As a leader and a researcher alike, it's important to avoid the trap of maintaining a constant narrative as against producing an accurate record. Did Grant set an example of being vulnerable in his career? Yes, he did.

In his book, *Think Again*, Grant dismisses his claims from his previous book, *Originals*, as simply wrong. Initially, he proposed that it pays to have 'strong opinions weekly held', but in the light of new research and his own findings, he pivoted to the stance that communicating an opining strongly often backfires.[35] What do you make of Grant as he rethinks: a better researcher or an underconfident one? I guess, you respect him even more now. But it takes courage, for what I came across in his book is still rare.

Marshall Goldsmith identifies four primary drivers of successful leadership: money, power, status and popularity.[36] The reason most others stop, and only a few persevere is that it becomes a zero-sum game after a point of time—you must win at the cost of somebody else. After all, how many CEOs can a company have at a given time? Or, can a team afford two captains? Hence, leaders behave very differently from their former selves once they reach that altitude. They have very high egos which are further exacerbated by constantly needing to be right. They have too much to lose by admitting being wrong, or even that they don't know. Eckhart noted that a complete identification with thoughts and emotions is ego, and most leaders often live in their heads.

You may claim that you are not that kind of a leader. And I trust you. But please don't become that, I urge. Anyway, it will be interesting for you to put the four—money, power, status, popularity—in your pecking order. It will be a useful exercise and will save you from a certain regret later in life.

The question then is: Why should a leader be vulnerable at all? And that too, by choice. If anything, she must be oozing overconfidence. That's what perhaps got her thus far. So why risk such a drastic change? And yet most leaders will agree that behavioural change is the *only* change that they can make at that level.

It's important that the leader doesn't fall for the trap that she has to innovate or that she must have the best ideas, or else she's phony. She neither has to be the smartest person in the room, nor the loudest. Even making her presence felt isn't always necessary. Here's a lesson in humility: When a child asked Walt Disney as to what exactly he did at the studio, he famously retorted, 'Well, sometimes I think of myself as a little bee. I go from one area of the studio to another and gather pollen and sort of stimulate everybody. I guess that's the job I do. I certainly don't consider myself a businessman, and I never did believe I was worth anything as an artist.'[37] If you are comfortable acknowledging and admitting that you are not the central piece of your universe, only then you develop people around you. Till such time, you are haunted by your own insecurities.

A leader is an embodiment of what others look up to following. If they have to act it out, it means they don't have it. In the swag of Bruce Lee, 'If you have to *think*, you still do not *understand*.'[38] Which means that being vulnerable by choice starts with developing content, competence and credibility for yourself. If you operate from a position of insecurity, how can others around you feel and behave any different? 'The mark of a champion is never the absence of fear or doubt, but rather how you respond when doubt and fear come a-calling,' notes the ultimate survivor, Bear Grylls. 'That's the clincher. Because if the stakes are high enough, trust me, the doubts and fears will come. What matters is how we respond.'[39] Acknowledge them and face them.

A leader must be vulnerable by choice and shouldn't come across as somebody who knows it all. People are generally smart enough to figure out how much you know. And if you are only left with the power of authority over them, and not power of knowledge or credibility, your days of power are finite. Marshall Goldsmith nails it down when he notes that being smart turns people on, but *announcing* how smart you are turns them off. And that's why there's a difference between an achiever and a leader—an achiever is self-centred whereas a leader is other-centred.

Satya Nadella, Microsoft CEO, offers some real instances of vulnerability. Barely a few months into his new role, Nadella was speaking at the Grace Hopper Celebration of Women in Computing event. The host probed Nadella on what actions he was taking to address the salary disparity of women in computing. Nadella said that women shouldn't worry about asking for raises, and should instead rely on 'good karma' and trust that the system would eventually reward their work. It didn't take him much criticism and time to realize that the question was posed to him in the capacity of the CEO of a tech company and not a question about his personal beliefs. Soon after, in an email to all Microsoft employees, Nadella admitted, 'I answered that question completely wrong.' He then went on to explain the steps the company was taking to address the disparity.[40]

It takes courage to firstly admit your mistake and secondly to write a public apology. How many leaders have you known who do that? If at all, they endlessly justify what they had said and wait for time to kill the memory. Barely six months into his new role, Nadella had a trial by fire, and he emerged triumphant. And this vulnerability by choice cemented his position not only as one of the world's best CEOs but also as an inspiration for the minorities in the tech industry.

The key to vulnerability is humility, and you demonstrate humility first by listening. 'Thinking you already know how a conversation will go down kills curiosity and subverts listening, as does anxiety about the interaction,' says Kate Murphy.[41] And most leaders are guilty of not letting others finish, even those who are not necessarily lower in the pecking order. A leader needs to be curious, courteous and attentive to sincerely reflect that she cares for you. And Kate is spot on when she observes that it's hard to develop the sensitivity and respect for another person's vulnerability without knowing what it's like to be vulnerable yourself.

Being vulnerable by choice also has a spiritual meaning. It relieves you of the pressure to guard your ego, which is, as you know by now, the source of most of your misery. As Eckhart put it, 'When you fully accept that you don't know, you actually enter a state of peace and clarity that is closer to who you truly are than thought could ever be.'[42]

Keep this in mind: You don't change once you become a leader. The causality is, in fact, the exact reverse.

Closing the book with some useful one-liners.

Appendix

Quotable Quotes from the Book

On living

- Life is long, pace it well.
- You may die accidentally, but you can't afford to live accidentally.
- Life doesn't always offer you what you ask for, but certainly gives you what you need.
- Be a lamp that glows well into the dark of the night than the spark that burns quickly and bright.
- 'It doesn't matter' means you surrender to the will of nature. You surrender *after* you have done your part and not before.
- Meditation is the gateway to being present in the moment, instead of regretting the past or contemplating the future.
- If you are adventurous enough to explore things in life, be humble enough to also forgive yourself and courageous enough to move to the next expedition.
- If you have a stable family and peace at home, you can conquer the world.

- The ability to radically cut down the chatter outside and within your head is the hallmark of disciplined living.
- Stop taking yourself too seriously (because nobody takes you seriously!).
- The biggest lesson the pandemic taught us is that life goes on with you or without you.

On thinking

- The evolution of your thinking is not a natural consequence of your career progression.
- Learn to ignore profusely, tolerate comfortably, and confront selectively.
- Keep a clear head to prioritize, a deep heart to empathize, and a thick skin to materialize.
- When you are not controlling your mind but rather are under complete control of your mind, it's a travesty.
- Fear not being alone with your thoughts, to synthesize, to conceptualize, to actualize, for in solitude you are least alone.

On working

- Financial freedom keeps you intellectually honest.
- Don't confuse being busy with being meaningful.
- You are not a resource to be consumed but rather an asset to be preserved.
- Seek love as a driver amid your fears, longings and responsibilities.

- Excellence is about doing the boring stuff well.
- Where you learn from needn't be where you earn from.
- There must be a better reason for your personal sacrifice than your professional growth.
- Passion is blind.
- Think of your career as actions to be taken rather than identities to be claimed.
- You are not your job; you are always more. Always.

On problem-solving

- Every problem is a symptom.
- A problem fully understood is half solved.
- If empathy is about understanding problems, creativity is about solving problems.
- You haven't learnt it unless it's in your veins.

On creativity and innovation

- Innovation calls for personal risk-taking. (PS: The key operative here is not risk).
- You won't be remembered for what you managed, but for what you created.
- Innovation is a political process. It's not the best idea that wins, but the most 'acceptable' one that does.
- If you are risking attempting even a slight amount of creativity, be ready to be ridiculed.
- Not experimenting is costly, and not experimenting, per say.

- Creativity is the yin and yang of order and chaos. Without chaos nothing evolves, and without order nothing stays.
- Let 'sorry' come rather easily than 'please'.

On strategy

- Own the outcome, not the plan.
- Just because you can, doesn't mean you should.
- You must plan but you can't be enslaved by the plan.
- Most firms don't go bust for a lack of operational efficiency but because of a want of directional clarity.
- Those who conserve and converge their attention on to significant issues get their names etched in the annals of time.
- The higher you go the broader you must look; else your elevation has little significance to self, or even to those around you.

On leadership

- Leaders fuel risk, managers contain risk.
- Leadership is not a popularity contest. It's about getting the extraordinary done through ordinary talent.
- If money can't motivate somebody and if the nature of the work can't motivate that person, then even you can't.
- A leader must be vulnerable by choice and shouldn't come across as somebody who knows it all.
- You don't change once you become a leader. The causality is, in fact, the exact reverse.

On technology

- Whenever machines get stronger, we humans get weaker.
- Technology is an obedient slave, but a tyrant master.
- Each new technology pushes you up the value chain.
- In the pursuit of making machines more like humans, we humans are becoming more like machines.

Notes

Chapter 1: Life Is Long, Pace It Well

1 Eckhart Tolle, *A New Earth: Creating a Better Life* (New York, N.Y.: Penguin Random House, 2005).

2 WorldOMeters, available at https://www.worldometers. info/demographics/india-demographics/#life-exp.

3 Phil Knight, *Shoe Dog: A Memoir by the Creator of Nike* (London, England: Simon & Schuster, 2016).

4 Meredith Somers, 'The 20-year-old entrepreneur is a lie', *Ideas Made to Matter*, 20 April 2018, available at https:// mitsloan.mit.edu/ideas-made-to-matter/20-year-old-entrepreneur-a-lie.

5 Rasmus Bjørk, 'The age at which Noble Prize research is conducted', *Scientometrics*, 2 March 2019.

6 Khalil Gibran, *The Prophet* (New York: Alfred A. Knopf, 1923).

7 Bruce Lee and John R. Little, *Striking Thoughts: Bruce Lee's Wisdom for Daily Living* (Boston, Mass.: Tuttle Publishing, 2002).

8 Jiddu Krishnamurti, *Freedom from the Known* (London: Rider Books, 1969).

9   Bruce Lee and John R. Little, *Striking Thoughts: Bruce Lee's Wisdom for Daily Living* (Boston, Mass.: Tuttle Publishing, 2002).

10   Richard P. Feynman, *'Surely You're Joking, Mr Feynman!': Adventures of a Curious Character as told to Ralph Leighton* (New York: W.W. Norton & Company, 1985).

11   Thomas Levenson, 'The Truth About Isaac Newton's Productive Plague', *New Yorker*, 6 April 2020, available at https://www.newyorker.com/culture/cultural-comment/the-truth-about-isaac-newtons-productive-plague.

12   Rafael Nadal and John Carlin, *Rafa: My Story* (London: Sphere, 2011).

13   Ibid.

14   Ibid.

15   Indra Nooyi, *My Life in Full: Work, Family, and Our Future* (Gurugram, India: Hachette India, 2021).

16   Nikola Tesla and Ben Johnston, *My Inventions: The Autobiography of Nikola Tesla* (Williston, Vt.: Hart Bros., 1982).

17   Ashlee Vance, *Elon Musk: Tesla, SpaceX, and the Quest for a Fantastic Future* (New York, NY: Penguin Random House, 2015).

18   George Ojemann, Jeff Ojemann, E. Lettich, and Mitchel Berger, 'Cortical language localization in left, dominant hemisphere: An electrical stimulation mapping investigation in 117 patients', *Journal of Neurosurgery* (1989).

19   'If Beethoven was completely deaf, how did he compose music?', *Classic FM*, 7 March 2023, available at https://www.classicfm.com/composers/beethoven/guides/deaf-hearing-loss-composing.

20   Ludwig van Beethoven, *British Library*, available at https://www.bl.uk/people/ludwig-van-beethoven.

21 Rachel Sylvester, '"Dyslexia Is My Superpower": How Learning Differently Helped Richard Branson Become a Rule-Breaking Billionaire', *RobbReport*, 18 July 2022, available at https://robbreport.com/lifestyle/news/richard-branson-dyslexia-1234727547/.

22 Eckhart Tolle, *A New Earth: Creating a Better Life* (New York, N.Y.: Penguin Random House, 2005).

23 Bear Grylls, *Never Give Up: A Life of Adventure* (London: Penguin Random House, 2021).

24 'The Big Lebowski | Bowling With "The Jesus"', YouTube.com, 22 May 2022, available at https://www.youtube.com/watch?v=YPfdSu6wO08.

25 'Troy (Achilles Vs Boagrius) 4K', YouTube.com, 22 May 2022, available at https://www.youtube.com/watch?v=_z5UKystdZg.

26 'Focusing is about saying no', Steve Jobs (WWDC 1997), YouTube.com, 26 January 2011, available at https://www.youtube.com/watch?v=H8eP99neOVs.

27 'General Electric announces plan to split into three separate companies', *The Guardian*, 9 November 2021, available at https://www.theguardian.com/business/2021/nov/09/general-electric-business-healthcare-energy-aviation.

28 'Nadella Says Children's Challenges Taught Him Empathy', YouTube.com, 25 October 2017, available at https://www.youtube.com/watch?v=SbAPmVoWVZs.

29 Simon Mundy and Victor Mallet, 'Tata boss: "I needed to stop the bleeding"', *Financial Times*, 19 February 2018, available at https://www.ft.com/content/b2c39d0c-1194-11e8-940e-08320fc2a277.

30 Elizabeth Gilbert, *Big Magic: Creative Living Beyond Fear* (London: Bloomsbury, 2015).

31 Richard P. Feynman, *'Surely You're Joking, Mr Feynman!'*: *Adventures of a Curious Character as told to Ralph Leighton* (New York: W.W. Norton & Company, 1985).

32 Ibid.

33 Ibid.

34 Paul Kalanithi, *When Breath Becomes Air* (New York: Penguin Random House, 2016).

35 Khalil Gibran, *The Prophet* (New York: Alfred A. Knopf, 1923).

36 His Holiness the Dalai Lama, *My Spiritual Autobiography* (London: Rider, 2012).

37 Eckhart Tolle, *A New Earth: Creating a Better Life* (New York, N.Y.: Penguin Random House, 2005).

38 'The Daily Show, Roger Federer - Tennis Legend | The Daily Show', Youtube.com, 8 December 2022, available at https://www.youtube.com/watch?v=W6rKB_UxONE.

39 'Air & Space Forces Association, Jeff Bezos Interview with AFA President Gen. Larry Spencer, Ret.', Youtube.com, available at https://www.youtube.com/watch?v=NSzdCAt8phE.

Chapter 2: Deserve before Your Desire

1 Viktor E. Frankl, *Man's Search for Meaning: The Classis Tribute to Hope from the Holocaust* (Boston: Beacon Press, 1992).

2 Yuval Noah Harari, *21 Lessons for the 21st Century* (London: Penguin Random House, 2018).

3 Eckhart Tolle, *A New Earth: Creating a Better Life* (New York, N.Y.: Penguin Random House, 2005).

4 Yuval Noah Harari, *21 Lessons for the 21st Century* (London: Penguin Random House, 2018).

5 Bruce Weber, 'Swift and Slashing, Computer Topples Kasparov', *The New York Times*, 12 May 1997, available at https://www.nytimes.com/1997/05/12/nyregion/swift-and-slashing-computer-topples-kasparov.

6 Amit Karmarkar, 'How India became a country of chess grandmasters', *The Times of India*, 24 January 2023, available at https://timesofindia.indiatimes.com/india/how-india-built-second-biggest-army-of-gms-in-35-years/articleshow/97176031.cms.

7 Viswanathan Anand, *Mind Master: Winning Lessons from a Champion's Life* (Gurugram, India: Hachette India, 2019).

8 Eric Schmidt, 'Eric Schmidt: This is how AI will transform the way science gets done', *MIT Technology Review*, 5 July 2023, available at https://www.technologyreview.com/2023/07/05/1075865/eric-schmidt-ai-will-transform-science/.

9 Jiddu Krishnamurti, *Freedom from the Known* (London: Rider Books, 1969).

10 Eckhart Tolle, *A New Earth: Creating a Better Life* (New York, N.Y.: Penguin Random House, 2005).

11 Annette Simmons, *The Story Factor: Inspiration, Influence, and Persuasion through the Art of Storytelling* (New York: Basic Books, 2019).

12 Viswanathan Anand, *Mind Master: Winning Lessons from a Champion's Life* (Gurugram, India: Hachette India, 2019).

13 Bruce Lee and John R. Little, *Striking Thoughts: Bruce Lee's Wisdom for Daily Living* (Boston, Mass.: Tuttle Publishing, 2002).

14 'Study Suggests Medical Errors Now Third Leading Cause of Death in the U.S.', *Johns Hopkins Medicine*, 3 May 2016, available at https://www.hopkinsmedicine.org/

news/media/releases/study_suggests_medical_errors_now_
third_leading_cause_of_death_in_the_us.

15 'Doctor Saved Michigan $100 Million', *NPR*, 9 December
2007, available at https://www.npr.org/templates/story/
story.php?storyId=17060374.

16 Atul Gawande, *The Checklist Manifesto: How to Get Things
Right* (New York, N.Y.: Metropolitan Books, 2009).

17 Ibid.

18 'Krishnamurti Foundation Trust, Computers are taking
over | Krishnamurti', 30 April 2022, Youtube.com, available
at https://www.youtube.com/watch?v=0qfda11Nv_0.

19 Thich Nhat Hanh, *The Miracle of Mindfulness: The Classic
Guide* (Boston: Beacon Press, 1987).

20 Jiddu Krishnamurti, *Freedom from the Known* (London:
Rider Books, 1969).

21 'David Rubenstein, Bridgewater's Ray Dalio on The David
Rubenstein Show', Youtube.com, 3 February 2022, available
at https://www.youtube.com/watch?v=jgb29wBy2kU.

22 Ezra Klein, 'Yuval Harari, author of Sapiens, on how
meditation made him a better historian', The Gray
Area, 28 February 2017, available at https://www.vox.
com/2017/2/28/14745596/yuval-harari-sapiens-interview-
meditation-ezra-klein.

23 John Medina, *Brain Rules: 12 Principles for Surviving and
Thriving at Work, Home, and School* (Seattle, WA: Pear
Press, 2009).

24 Daniel Goleman, 'What makes a Leader?', *Harvard Business
Review*, January 2004.

25 His Holiness the Dalai Lama, *My Spiritual Autobiography*
(London: Rider, 2012).

26 Marshall   Goldsmith,   'Displaying   Your   Singular
Empathy', *Marshall Goldsmith Blog*, available at https://

marshallgoldsmith.com/articles/displaying-your-singular-empathy/.

27 Satya Nadella, *Hit Refresh: The Quest to Rediscover Microsoft's Soul and Imagine a Better Future for Everyone* (New York: Harper Business, 2017).

28 Kate Murphy, *You're Not Listening: What You're Missing & Why It Matters* (New York: Celadon Books, 2021).

29 Khalil Gibran, *The Prophet* (New York: Alfred A. Knopf, 1923).

30 Jordan B. Peterson, *12 Rules for Life: An Antidote to Chaos* (London: Penguin Random House, 2018).

31 Rebecca Ackermann, 'Design thinking was supposed to fix the world. Where did it go wrong?', *MIT Technology Review*, 9 February 2023, available at https://www.technologyreview.com/2023/02/09/1067821/design-thinking-retrospective-what-went-wrong/.

32 Marshall Goldsmith, 'Displaying Your Singular Empathy', *Marshall Goldsmith Blog*, available at https://marshallgoldsmith.com/articles/displaying-your-singular-empathy/.

33 Paul Kalanithi, *When Breath Becomes Air* (New York: Penguin Random House, 2016).

34 Yuval Noah Harari, *21 Lessons for the 21st Century* (London: Penguin Random House, 2018).

35 Bruce Lee and John R. Little, *Striking Thoughts: Bruce Lee's Wisdom for Daily Living* (Boston, Mass.: Tuttle Publishing, 2002).

36 Phil Knight, *Shoe Dog: A Memoir by the Creator of Nike* (London, England: Simon & Schuster, 2016).

37 Ford, H., Crowther, S. and Woodrow Wilson Collection, *My Life and Work* (Garden City, N.Y., Doubleday, Page & Company, 1922).

38 'Failing for Success: Henry A. Ford', *Intellectual Ventures*, 2 August 2016, available at https://www.intellectualventures.com/buzz/insights/failing-for-success-henry-a.-ford.

39 John Medina, *Brain Rules: 12 Principles for Surviving and Thriving at Work, Home, and School* (Seattle, WA: Pear Press, 2009).

40 Walter Isaacson, *Einstein: His Life and Universe* (New York: Simon & Schuster, 2007).

41 Gary Wolf, 'Steve Jobs: The Next Insanely Great Thing', *Wired*, 1 February 1996, available at https://www.wired.com/1996/02/jobs-2/.

42 Jeff Bezos, '2018 Letter to Shareholders', Amazon.com, 11 April 2019, available at https://www.aboutamazon.com/news/company-news/2018-letter-to-shareholders.

43 'Air & Space Forces Association, Jeff Bezos' Interview with AFA President Gen. Larry Spencer, Ret.', Youtube.com, available at https://www.youtube.com/watch?v=NSzdCAt8phE.

44 Elizabeth Gilbert, *Big Magic: Creative Living Beyond Fear* (London: Bloomsbury, 2015).

45 Adam Grant, *Think Again: The Power of Knowing What You Don't Know* (New York: Penguin Random House, 2021).

46 'Air & Space Forces Association, Jeff Bezos' Interview with AFA President Gen. Larry Spencer, Ret.', Youtube.com, available at https://www.youtube.com/watch?v=NSzdCAt8phE.

47 Jeff Bezos, '2018 Letter to Shareholders', Amazon.com, 11 April 2019, available at https://www.aboutamazon.com/news/company-news/2018-letter-to-shareholders.

48 David Pierce, 'How Google Goggles Won, Then Lost, the Camera-First Future', *Wired*, 27 October 2017, available at https://www.wired.com/story/from-google-goggles-to-google-lens/.

49   Satya Nadella, *Hit Refresh: The Quest to Rediscover Microsoft's Soul and Imagine a Better Future for Everyone* (New York: Harper Business, 2017).

50   Jeff Bezos, '2018 Letter to Shareholders', Amazon.com, 11 April 2019, available at https://www.aboutamazon.com/news/company-news/2018-letter-to-shareholders.

51   Sambit Bal, 'The birth of reverse swing', *ESPN Cricinfo*, 1 March 2005, available at https://www.espncricinfo.com/story/the-birth-of-reverse-swing-145722.

52   Team Sportstar, 'The story of Dhoni being made India captain for 2007 World T20', *The Hindu*, 28 June 2022, available at https://sportstar.thehindu.com/cricket/dhoni-2007-t20-world-cup-captain-tendulkar-srinivasan-ipl/article65598552.ece.

53   Robin Sharma, *The Monk Who Sold His Ferrari: A Fable About Fulfilling Your Dreams and Reaching Your Destiny* (Toronto: HarperCollins, 1998).

54   Michael Simmons, 'Bill Gates, Warren Buffett, and Oprah all use the 5-hour rule. Here's how this powerful habit works', *Business Insider*, 25 February 2020, available at https://www.businessinsider.com/bill-gates-warren-buffet-and-oprah-all-use-the-5-hour-rule-2017-7.

55   Elizabeth Gilbert, *Big Magic: Creative Living Beyond Fear* (London: Bloomsbury, 2015).

56   Eckhart Tolle, *A New Earth: Creating a Better Life* (New York, N.Y.: Penguin Random House, 2005).

57   Richard P. Feynman, *'Surely You're Joking, Mr Feynman!': Adventures of a Curious Character as told to Ralph Leighton* (New York: W.W. Norton & Company, 1985).

58   John Medina, *Brain Rules: 12 Principles for Surviving and Thriving at Work, Home, and School* (Seattle, WA: Pear Press, 2009).

59 David Epstein, *Range: Why Generalists Triumph in a Specialized World* (New York: Riverhead Books, 2019).

60 Viswanathan Anand, *Mind Master: Winning Lessons from a Champion's Life* (Gurugram, India: Hachette India, 2019).

61 Paul Kalanithi, *When Breath Becomes Air* (New York: Penguin Random House, 2016).

62 Ian Cross, 'Music, cognition, culture, and evolution', *Annals of the New York Academy of Sciences*, (2001).

63 John Medina, *Brain Rules: 12 Principles for Surviving and Thriving at Work, Home, and School* (Seattle, WA: Pear Press, 2009).

64 Michael Balter, Closer Look at Einstein's Brain, *Science*, 17 Apil 2009, available at https://www.science.org/content/article/closer-look-einsteins-brain.

65 Lemelson-MIT, available at https://lemelson.mit.edu/resources/thomas-edison.

66 Scotty Hendricks, 'The hobbies of 5 great geniuses', *Big Think*, 6 December 2022, available at https://bigthink.com/the-past/hobbies-five-great-geniuses.

67 Nassim Nicholas Taleb, *Skin in the Game: Hidden Asymmetries of Daily Life* (New York: Random House, 2018).

68 Phil Knight, *Shoe Dog: A Memoir by the Creator of Nike* (London, England: Simon & Schuster, 2016).

69 Elizabeth Gilbert, *Big Magic: Creative Living Beyond Fear* (London: Bloomsbury, 2015).

70 M. Scott Peck, *The Road Less Travelled* (New York: Simon and Schuster, 1978).

71 Lovetennis, 'When Martina Hingis taught Roger Federer about discipline', 29 May 2021, available at https://www.lovetennis.com/grand-slam/when-martina-hingis-taught-roger-federer-about-discipline/.

72 'Andy Roddick interviews Roger Federer', YouTube. com, available at https://www.youtube.com/watch?v=_ sBZ47tnCDk.

73 David Rubenstein, 'Amazon CEO Jeff Bezos on The David Rubenstein Show', YouTube, 19 September 2018, https:// www.youtube.com/watch?v=f3NBQcAqyu4.

74 Jonathan Amos, 'Why India's Mars mission is so cheap - and thrilling', *BBC News*, 24 September 2014, available at https:// www.bbc.com/news/science-environment-29341850.

75 R. Aravamudan, *ISRO: A Personal History* (Noida, India: HarperCollins, 2017).

76 Ibid.

77 BAFTA Guru, '"It's really about sticking to your guns"' | Christopher Nolan on Directing', YouTube.com, 18 January 2018, available at https://www.youtube.com/ watch?v=0CaDZamA2ok.

78 Sam Walton and John Huey, *Made in America: My Story* (New York: Bantam Books, 1992).

79 Eckhart Tolle, *A New Earth: Creating a Better Life* (New York, N.Y.: Penguin Random House, 2005).

80 Kate Murphy, *You're Not Listening: What You're Missing & Why It Matters* (New York: Celadon Books, 2021).

81 Jiddu Krishnamurti, *Freedom from the Known* (London: Rider Books, 1969).

Chapter 3: Own Your Career, or Somebody Else Will

1 M. Scott Peck, *The Road Less Travelled* (New York: Simon and Schuster, 1978).

2 Steven Maier and Martin Seligman, 'Learned Helplessness: Theory and Evidence', *Journal of Experimental Psychology* (1976).

3   Pavan Lall, 'The force is with Arundhati', *Fortune India*,
    30 November 2020, available at https://www.fortuneindia.
    com/people/the-force-is-with-arundhati/104870.

4   Investor Archive, 'Warren Buffett | HBO Documentary',
    YouTube.com, 10 November 2020, available at https://
    www.youtube.com/watch?v=e89nA8glj3U.

5   Paul Kalanithi, *When Breath Becomes Air* (New York:
    Penguin Random House, 2016).

6   John Medina, *Brain Rules: 12 Principles for Surviving and
    Thriving at Work, Home, and School* (Seattle, WA: Pear
    Press, 2009).

7   Alexandra Vaccaro and Yosef Kaplan Dor, 'Why Severe
    Sleep Deprivation Can be Lethal', *Harvard Brain Science
    Initiative*, 11 June 2020, available at https://brain.harvard.
    edu/hbi_news/why-severe-sleep-deprivation-can-be-
    lethal/.

8   David Rubenstein, 'Amazon CEO Jeff Bezos on
    The David Rubenstein Show', YouTube.com, 19
    September 2018, available at https://www.youtube.com/
    watch?v=f3NBQcAqyu4.

9   Ashton Jackson, 'Elon Musk says he's upped his sleep
    to 6 hours per night—and that his old routine hurt his
    brain', *CNBC*, 18 May 2023, available at https://www.
    cnbc.com/2023/05/18/elon-musk-sacrificing-sleep-for-
    productivity-gave-me-brain-pain.html.

10 Blake Stilwell, 'Here's what NASA says is the perfect
    length for a power nap', *Business Insider*, 26 March 2019,
    available at https://www.businessinsider.in/thelife/heres-
    what-nasa-says-is-the-perfect-length-for-a-power-nap/
    articleshow/68570353.cms.

11 'Benefits of Exercise', *NHS*, 4 August 2021, available at
    https://www.nhs.uk/live-well/exercise/exercise-health-
    benefits/.

12 John Medina, *Brain Rules: 12 Principles for Surviving and Thriving at Work, Home, and School* (Seattle, WA: Pear Press, 2009).

13 Robin Sharma, *The Monk Who Sold His Ferrari: A Fable About Fulfilling Your Dreams and Reaching Your Destiny* (Toronto: HarperCollins, 1998).

14 Khalil Gibran, *The Prophet* (New York: Alfred A. Knopf, 1923).

15 Jiddu Krishnamurti, *Freedom from the Known* (London: Rider Books, 1969).

16 Satya Nadella, *Hit Refresh: The Quest to Rediscover Microsoft's Soul and Imagine a Better Future for Everyone* (New York: Harper Business, 2017).

17 Bill Gates, 'This book left me in tears', *GatesNotes*, 7 March 2017, available at https://www.gatesnotes.com/When-Breath-Becomes-Air.

18 Paul Kalanithi, *When Breath Becomes Air* (New York: Penguin Random House, 2016).

19 VICE, 'Christopher Nolan on "Following" - Conversations Inside The Criterion Collection', YouTube.com, 24 August 2014, available at https://www.youtube.com/watch?v=jUpA7Qma_9E.

20 Sam Walton and John Huey, *Made in America: My Story* (New York: Bantam Books, 1992).

21 Sai Mohapatra, 'I've never wanted to prove anything to anyone', ESPN Cricinfo, 11 July 2012, available at https://www.espncricinfo.com/story/sachin-tendulkar-i-ve-never-wanted-to-prove-anything-to-anyone-571796.

22 Anita Bhogle and Harsha Bhogle, *The Winning Way: Learnings from Sports for Managers* (Chennai, India: Westland Ltd., 2011).

23 'Dhoni To Commence Patrolling, Guard Duties With 106 Para TA Battalion in Kashmir Valley From Today',

ABPLive.com, 31 July 2019, available at https://news.abplive.com/sports/cricket/ms-dhoni-to-commence-patrolling-guard-duties-with-106-para-ta-battalion-in-insurgency-hit-kashmir-valley-1223656.

24 Shilarze Saharoy, 'Indian army veteran says the armed forces have missed out on a good officer in Mahendra Singh Dhoni', *The Times of India*, 7 July 2020, available at https://timesofindia.indiatimes.com/sports/off-the-field/indian-army-veteran-says-the-armed-forces-might-have-missed-out-on-a-good-officer-in-mahendra-singh-dhoni/articleshow/76829739.cms.

25 Carol Breckenridge, 'Art as Therapy: How Churchill Coped', *International Churchill Society*, available at https://winstonchurchill.org/publications/finest-hour/finest-hour-120/art-as-therapy-how-churchill-coped/.

26 Angela Duckworth, *Grit: The Power of Passion and Perseverance* (New York: Simon & Schuster, 2016).

27 Adam Grant, *Think Again: The Power of Knowing What You Don't Know* (New York: Penguin Random House, 2021).

28 Nassim Nicholas Taleb, *Skin in the Game: Hidden Asymmetries of Daily Life* (New York: Random House, 2018).

29 Yuval Noah Harari, *21 Lessons for the 21st Century* (London: Penguin Random House, 2018).

30 Phil Knight, *Shoe Dog: A Memoir by the Creator of Nike* (London, England: Simon & Schuster, 2016).

31 Rafael Nadal and John Carlin, *Rafa: My Story* (London: Sphere, 2011).

32 Adam Grant, *Think Again: The Power of Knowing What You Don't Know* (New York: Penguin Random House, 2021).

33 Jeff Bezos, '2018 Letter to Shareholders', Amazon.com, 11 April 2019, available at https://www.aboutamazon.com/news/company-news/2018-letter-to-shareholders.

34 *Nassim Nicholas Taleb, Skin in the Game: Hidden Asymmetries of Daily Life* (New York: Random House, 2018).

35 Elizabeth Gilbert, *Big Magic: Creative Living Beyond Fear* (London: Bloomsbury, 2015).

36 Jiddu Krishnamurti, *Freedom from the Known* (London: Rider Books, 1969).

37 Mitch Albom, *Tuesdays with Morrie: An Old Man, a Young Man, and Life's Greatest Lesson* (New York: Doubleday, 1997).

38 Bruce Lee and John R. Little, *Striking Thoughts: Bruce Lee's Wisdom for Daily Living* (Boston, Mass.: Tuttle Publishing, 2002).

39 Shiv Aroor and Rahul Singh, *India's Most Fearless 1: True Stories of Modern Military Heroes* (Gurugram, India: Penguin Random House, 2017).

40 Vayu Sena Medal Awardee List for the year 2017, *Bharat Rakshak*, available at https://www.bharat-rakshak.com/IAF/Database/Awards.

Chapter 4: Focus on High Leverage Activities

1 Jim Collins, *Good to Great: Why Some Companies Make the Leap . . . and Others Don't* (London, England: Random House Business Books, 2001).

2 Naval Ravikant, *Naval*, 24 May 2019, available at https://nav.al/productize-yourself.

3 Bharat Sundaresan, *The Dhoni Touch* (Gurugram, India: Penguin Random House, 2018).

4   Farnam Street, 'Understanding your Circle of Competence:
    How Warren Buffett Avoids Problems', available at https://
    fs.blog/circle-of-competence.
5   Marshall Goldsmith, *What Got You Here Won't Get You
    There* (London: Profile Books Limited, 2008).
6   Viktor E. Frankl, *Man's Search for Meaning: The Classis
    Tribute to Hope from the Holocaust* (Boston: Beacon Press,
    1992).
7   Bear Grylls, *True Grit* (London: Bantam Press, 2013).
8   Mihaly Csikszentmihalyi, *Flow: The Classic Works on How
    to Achieve Happiness* (New York: Harper & Row, 1992).
9   Robin Sharma, *The Monk Who Sold His Ferrari: A Fable
    About Fulfilling Your Dreams and Reaching Your Destiny*
    (Toronto: HarperCollins, 1998).
10 A.P.J. Abdul Kalam, *Wings of Fire: An Autobiography*
    (Hyderabad, India: Universities Press, 1999).
11 Jiddu Krishnamurti, *Freedom from the Known* (London:
    Rider Books, 1969).
12 Bruce Lee and John R. Little, *Striking Thoughts: Bruce Lee's
    Wisdom for Daily Living* (Boston, Mass.: Tuttle Publishing,
    2002).
13 Jocko Willink and Leif Babin, *Extreme Ownership: How
    U.S. Navy SEALs Lead and Win* (New York: St Martin's
    Publishing Group, 2017).
14 Satya Nadella, *Hit Refresh: The Quest to Rediscover Microsoft's
    Soul and Imagine a Better Future for Everyone* (New York:
    Harper Business, 2017).
15 Nikola Tesla and Ben Johnston, *My Inventions: The
    Autobiography of Nikola Tesla* (Williston, Vt.: Hart Bros.,
    1982).
16 David Epstein, *Range: Why Generalists Triumph in a
    Specialized World* (New York: Riverhead Books, 2019).

17 M. Scott Peck, *The Road Less Travelled* (New York: Simon and Schuster, 1978).

18 Eckhart Tolle, *A New Earth: Creating a Better Life* (New York, N.Y.: Penguin Random House, 2005).

19 John Snow, Cholera, 'The Broad Street Pump: Waterborne Diseases Then and Now', *National Library of Medicine*, 30 March 2018, available at https://www.ncbi.nlm.nih.gov/pmc/articles/PMC7150208/.

20 Yuval Noah Harari, *21 Lessons for the 21st Century* (London: Penguin Random House, 2018).

21 'Leadership Tips From the President Himself | Bill Clinton @ LEAD presented by HR.com', YouTube.com, available at https://www.youtube.com/watch?v=h198ZlfXViA.

22 Annette Simmons, *The Story Factor: Inspiration, Influence, and Persuasion through the Art of Storytelling* (New York: Basic Books, 2019).

23 Barbara Minto, *The Minto Pyramid Principle: Logic in Writing, Thinking, and Problem Solving* (London: Financial Times Prentice Hall, 2002).

24 McKinsey Alumni Centre, 'Barbara Minto: "MECE: I invented it, so I get to say how to pronounce it"', available at https://www.mckinsey.com/alumni/news-and-events/global-news/alumni-news/barbara-minto-mece-i-invented-it-so-i-get-to-say-how-to-pronounce-it.

25 Bruce Lee and John R. Little, *Striking Thoughts: Bruce Lee's Wisdom for Daily Living* (Boston, Mass.: Tuttle Publishing, 2002).

Chapter 5: Think Strategically, Act Decisively

1 A.P.J. Abdul Kalam, *Wings of Fire: An Autobiography* (Hyderabad, India: Universities Press, 1999).

2   Shiv Aroor and Rahul Singh, *India's Most Fearless 1: True Stories of Modern Military Heroes* (Gurugram, India: Penguin Random House, 2017).

3   Jocko Willink and Leif Babin, *Extreme Ownership: How U.S. Navy SEALs Lead and Win* (New York: St Martin's Publishing Group, 2017).

4   Paul Kalanithi, *When Breath Becomes Air* (New York: Penguin Random House, 2016).

5   S. Jayashankar, *The India Way: Strategies for an Uncertain World* (Gurugram, India: HarperCollins, 2020).

6   Viswanathan Anand, *Mind Master: Winning Lessons from a Champion's Life* (Gurugram, India: Hachette India, 2019).

7   Satya Nadella, *Hit Refresh: The Quest to Rediscover Microsoft's Soul and Imagine a Better Future for Everyone* (New York: Harper Business, 2017).

8   Louis V. Gerstner, Jr, *Who Says Elephants Can't Dance?: Leading a Great Enterprise Through Dramatic Change* (New York: Harper Business, 2003).

9   The Quint, 'MS Dhoni On How He Controls His Emotions on the Cricket Field | *The Quint*', YouTube. com, 17 October 2019, available at https://www.youtube. com/watch?v=6sfNvXLHk18.

10 Bharat Sundaresan, *The Dhoni Touch* (Gurugram, India: Penguin Random House, 2018).

11 Marge Pamintuan Perko, 'To the Stars and Beyond', *News UC Santa Barbara*, 26 October 2015, available at https:// news.ucsb.edu/2015/016077/stars-and-beyond.

12 Farnam Street, 'Mental Models: The Best Way to Make Intelligent Decisions (~100 Models Explained)', available at https://fs.blog/mental-models/.

13 'Air & Space Forces Association, Jeff Bezos' Interview with AFA President Gen. Larry Spencer, Ret.', YouTube.com, available at https://www.youtube.com/watch?v=NSzdCAt8phE.

14 Satya Nadella, *Hit Refresh: The Quest to Rediscover Microsoft's Soul and Imagine a Better Future for Everyone* (New York: Harper Business, 2017).

15 Nassim Nicholas Taleb, *Skin in the Game: Hidden Asymmetries of Daily Life* (New York: Random House, 2018).

16 Winston Ibrahim–Minutes, 'Jeff Bezos uses a simple framework for making big decisions. Here's how it works', *FastCompany*, 8 May 2021, available at https://www.fastcompany.com/90662406/jeff-bezos-uses-a-simple-framework-for-making-big-decisions-heres-how-it-works.

17 'Air & Space Forces Association, Jeff Bezos Interview with AFA President Gen. Larry Spencer, Ret.', YouTube.com, available at https://www.youtube.com/watch?v=NSzdCAt8phE.

18 Rohin Dharmakumar, Seema Singh, and N.S. Ramnath, 'How Nandan Nilekani Took Aadhaar Past The Tipping Point', *Forbes India*, 8 October 2013, available at https://www.forbesindia.com/article/big-bet/how-nandan-nilekani-took-aadhaar-past-the-tipping-point/36259/1.

19 Shankkar Aiyar, 'History of Aadhaar: How Nandan's Core Team Came Together', *YourStory*, 13 July 2017, available at https://yourstory.com/2017/07/history-of-aadhaar.

20 Rohin Dharmakumar, Seema Singh, and N.S. Ramnath, 'How Nandan Nilekani Took Aadhaar Past The Tipping Point', *Forbes India*, 8 October 2013, available at https://www.forbesindia.com/article/big-bet/how-nandan-nilekani-took-aadhaar-past-the-tipping-point/36259/1.

21 Bruce Lee and John R. Little, *Striking Thoughts: Bruce Lee's Wisdom for Daily Living* (Boston, Mass.: Tuttle Publishing, 2002).

22 Khalil Gibran, *The Prophet* (New York: Alfred A. Knopf, 1923).

23   Phil Knight, *Shoe Dog: A Memoir by the Creator of Nike* (London, England: Simon & Schuster, 2016).

24   Laver Cup, 'Roger Federer & Rafael Nadal Interview | Laver Cup 2022', YouTube.com, 24 September 2022, available at https://www.youtube.com/watch?v=Y6_qFDijAac.

25   Air & Space Forces Association, 'Jeff Bezos' Interview with AFA President Gen. Larry Spencer, Ret.', YouTube.com, available at https://www.youtube.com/watch?v=NSzdCAt8phE.

26   Karen A. Jehn, *A multimethod examination of the benefits and detriments of intragroup conflict*, (Administrative Science Quarterly, 1995).

27   Adam Grant, *Think Again: The Power of Knowing What You Don't Know* (New York: Penguin Random House, 2021).

28   Robin Sharma, *The Monk Who Sold His Ferrari: A Fable About Fulfilling Your Dreams and Reaching Your Destiny* (Toronto: HarperCollins, 1998).

29   Edwin Markham, *The Gates of Paradise and Other Poems* (1928), available at https://www.poetryfoundation.org/poems/47959/preparedness

Chapter 6: Leadership Is a Choice Not Everyone Can Make

1   Jocko Willink and Leif Babin, *Extreme Ownership: How U.S. Navy SEALs Lead and Win* (New York: St Martin's Publishing Group, 2017).

2   'Abdul Kalam inspirational Speech on Leadership and Motivation', OneChannelIndia, available at https://www.youtube.com/watch?v=uHIWOf1H6tI.

3   Jim Collins, *Good to Great: Why Some Companies Make the Leap . . . and Others Don't* (London, England: Random House Business Books, 2001).

4   Shantanu Narayen, 'Adobe's CEO on Making Big Bets on Innovation', *Harvard Business Review*, November-December 2023, available at https://hbr.org/2023/11/adobes-ceo-on-making-big-bets-on-innovation.

5   'Leadership Tips From the President Himself | Bill Clinton @ LEAD Presented by HR.com', YouTube.com, available at https://www.youtube.com/watch?v=h198ZlfXViA.

6   R. Aravamudan, *ISRO: A Personal History* (Noida, India: HarperCollins, 2017).

7   Ibid.

8   List of PSLV Launches, available at https://www.isro.gov.in/PSLV_Launchers.html.

9   List of launch vehicle missions from Sriharikota, available at https://www.shar.gov.in/sdscshar/launchvehiclescompleted.jsp.

10 Warren Bennis and Patricia Ward Biederman, *Organizing Genius: The Secrets of Creative Collaboration* (Reading, Mass.: Addison-Wesley, 1997).

11 'Leadership Lecture Sam Manekshaw', YouTube.com, 28 Marh 2016, available at https://www.youtube.com/watch?v=eSvLFPFXjc8 .

12 'A life lived such - Field Marshal Sam Manekshaw', YouTube.com, 20 January 2013, available at https://www.youtube.com/watch?v=qRmPmm7QeIE.

13 Ibid.

14 Warren Bennis and Patricia Ward Biederman, *Organizing Genius: The Secrets of Creative Collaboration* (Reading, Mass.: Addison-Wesley, 1997).

15 Phil Knight, *Shoe Dog: A Memoir by the Creator of Nike* (London, England: Simon & Schuster, 2016).

16 Ashlee Vance, *Elon Musk: Tesla, SpaceX, and the Quest for a Fantastic Future* (New York, NY: Penguin Random House, 2015).

17 VICE, 'Christopher Nolan on "Following" - Conversations Inside The Criterion Collection', YouTube.com, 24 August 2014, available at https://www.youtube.com/watch?v=jUpA7Qma_9E.

18 Warren Bennis and Patricia Ward Biederman, *Organizing Genius: The Secrets of Creative Collaboration* (Reading, Mass.: Addison-Wesley, 1997).

19 Ashlee Vance, *Elon Musk: Tesla, SpaceX, and the Quest for a Fantastic Future* (New York, NY: Penguin Random House, 2015).

20 Stephen Clark, 'Sweet success at last for Falcon 1 rocket', *Spaceflight Now*, 28 September 2008, available at https://spaceflightnow.com/falcon/004/index.html.

21 Amy C. Edmondson, 'Leading in tough times', Harvard Business School, 22 November 2022, available at https://www.hbs.edu/recruiting/insights-and-advice/blog/post/leading-in-tough-times.

22 Ashlee Vance, *Elon Musk: Tesla, SpaceX, and the Quest for a Fantastic Future* (New York, NY: Penguin Random House, 2015).

23 Lockheed Martin, 'Kelly's 14 Rules', available at https://www.lockheedmartin.com/content/dam/lockheed-martin/aero/photo/skunkworks/kellys-14-rules.pdf.

24 Warren Bennis and Patricia Ward Biederman, *Organizing Genius: The Secrets of Creative Collaboration* (Reading, Mass.: Addison-Wesley, 1997).

25   Leslie Berlin, 'You've Never Heard of Tech Legend Bob
     Taylor, But He Invented "Almost Everything"', *Wired*, 21
     April 2017, available at https://www.wired.com/2017/04/
     youve-never-heard-tech-legend-bob-taylor-invented-
     almost-everything/.

26   Sam Walton and John Huey, *Made in America: My Story*
     (New York: Bantam Books, 1992).

27   Warren Bennis and Patricia Ward Biederman, *Organizing
     Genius: The Secrets of Creative Collaboration* (Reading,
     Mass.: Addison-Wesley, 1997).

28   Marshall Goldsmith, *What Got You Here Won't Get You
     There* (London: Profile Books Limited, 2008).

29   M. Scott Peck, *The Road Less Travelled* (New York: Simon
     and Schuster, 1978).

30   Jared Diamond, *Guns, Germs and Steel.* (London, England:
     Vintage, 1998).

31   Richard Thaler and Cass R. Sunstein, *Nudge: Improving
     Decisions about Health, Wealth, and Happiness* (New York:
     Penguin Random House, 2008).

32   Ashlee Vance, *Elon Musk: Tesla, SpaceX, and the Quest for a
     Fantastic Future* (New York, NY: Penguin Random House,
     2015).

33   Marshall Goldsmith, *What Got You Here Won't Get You
     There* (London: Profile Books Limited, 2008).

34   Adam Grant, *Think Again: The Power of Knowing What You
     Don't Know* (New York: Penguin Random House, 2021).

35   Ibid.

36   Marshall Goldsmith, *What Got You Here Won't Get You
     There* (London: Profile Books Limited, 2008).

37   Warren Bennis and Patricia Ward Biederman, *Organizing
     Genius: The Secrets of Creative Collaboration* (Reading,
     Mass.: Addison-Wesley, 1997).

38   Bruce Lee and John R. Little, *Striking Thoughts: Bruce Lee's Wisdom for Daily Living* (Boston, Mass.: Tuttle Publishing, 2002).

39   Bear Grylls, *Never Give Up: A Life of Adventure* (London: Penguin Random House, 2021).

40   Microsoft News Center, 'Satya Nadella email to employees: RE: Grace Hopper Conference', Microsoft, 9 October 2014, available at https://news.microsoft.com/2014/10/09/satya-nadella-email-to-employees-re-grace-hopper-conference/.

41   Kate Murphy, *You're Not Listening: What You're Missing & Why It Matters* (New York: Celadon Books, 2021).

42   Eckhart Tolle, *A New Earth: Creating a Better Life* (New York, N.Y.: Penguin Random House, 2005).

Index

Scan QR code to access the
Penguin Random House India website